SUPER AWARENESS

TECHNIQUES FOR TRANSFORMATION
& ENLIGHTENMENT

MARIA COWEN

Copyright © 2002 Maria Cowen
All rights reserved.
ISBN: 978-0-9906228-1-9

All rights reserved. No part of this book may be reproduced or transmitted in any form or by any means, electronic or mechanical, including photocopying, recording, or any information storage and retrieval system without prior written permission of the Author. Your support of Author's rights is appreciated.

Though this book is based on actual events, many names, dates, and locations have been changed to preserve the privacy of the participants.

relentlessly, and causes all the pain and problems in your life. Learn how to control this villain and expose it to reality.

CHAPTER TWO 17

Will acquaint you with the real aspect of you, the True self. Its existence is also a mystery to you, but once you reclaim its realization in consciousness your whole life transforms. This is no wispy, mystical concept ... it lives and breathes and is closer than your very thoughts or emotions.

CHAPTER THREE 29

The secret of the ages is revealed here. The Witness is your magic carpet on the journey to transformation and enlightenment. You will learn how to activate this part of your own consciousness; you will use its power of awareness to dissolve the stuff that holds you back. With the technique described, you will no longer suffer at your own hand.

CHAPTER FOUR 39

Self-observation and non-judgment are key concepts in the practical use of the Witness. Here you will learn to be more aware of your false self by watching its moods and reactions, then challenging its motives and actions ... this is the first step in detaching from Ego.

CHAPTER FIVE 47

The second part of the secret is revealed. Allowing and Non-resistance. Here you will learn of the force

TABLE OF CONTENTS

FOREWORD 1

The true enlightened man lives a simple and carefree life, he is **aware** in a way not normally understood, and he's practically invisible. He lives in a world almost opposite to that of his fellow beings. Where others thrive on the company and compliments of the crowd, he trusts only the wellspring of higher thought and empowered feelings that flow from within him. While others strive to excel and succeed, to be *someone*, he alone knows the power and satisfaction of being *no-one*, of being invisible.

INTRODUCTION 3

Explains "why" this system and hints at the nature of "enlightened" man.

CHAPTER ONE ....

Learn about the false self, the artificial personality that masquerades as you and you don't even know it. This entity steals your energy, drives you behind the Witness and how it exerts power on the things outside. These are no wimpy concepts. Once mastered, the world changes before your very eyes ... nothing will be the same again.

CHAPTER SIX 57

Higher Thought. Learn the difference between common everyday thought and the kind of thought that keeps your mind open and makes your heart fly. This is a further elaboration of former techniques that allow you to transform the old ... and enter a perfected realm where freedom is natural, growth is easy, and joy is abundant.

CHAPTER SEVEN 63

The Golden Path. Not the left-hand path of Science, nor the right-hand path of Religion, but instead, the middle way or golden mean. Learn to follow this path as an everyday practical approach. Life then becomes your classroom **and** your teacher.

CHAPTER EIGHT..71

Self-Transformation. Very powerful exercises and techniques, never before seen, designed for everyday use. Real transformation takes place on both the mental level and the physical. These are self-starters that accelerate your progress tenfold! Super Consciousness and full brain function become real possibilities.

CHAPTER NINE 85

Continues the previous information on Self-Transformation by uncovering the False Self's most guarded weapon for stealing your energy and keeping you constantly off balance. By knowing this secret, you disable the whole artificial structure of this massive entity and unravel the pathways to its many facets.

CHAPTER TEN 93

Have you ever had one of those magical days where everything seemed to go your way? Unexpected opportunities just fell into your lap, and people—even strangers—showered you with uncommon attention and compliments. You knew that something unusual and rare was happening, but you didn't know what.

CONCLUSION 103

Discovering one's personal truth is an ongoing process and is the most important pursuit in a person's life. Inner guidance must be trusted as infallible to steer one along the path of truth. What feels good is right; what feels bad is wrong (for you). Don't let the societal and religious concept of Conscience interfere -- anything done out of guilt or fear is wrong.

BIBLIOGRAPHY 115

FOREWORD

The true enlightened man lives a simple and carefree life, he is **aware** in a way not normally understood, and he's practically invisible. He lives in a world almost opposite to that of his fellow beings. Where others thrive on the company and compliments of the crowd, he trusts only the wellspring of higher thought and empowered feelings that flow from within him. While others strive to excel and succeed, to be *someone*, he alone knows the power and satisfaction of being *no-one*, of being invisible.

Do not misunderstand. This is not a philosophy for losers, but of real men and real women. It takes courage and discipline to lead a life out of step with the world at large. Anyone who's tried to do it alone against the tide of simple peer pressure will recognize the difficulty involved. Those who persevere, however, will gain treasures beyond belief.

The common man has been tragically deceived. He's been taught to misuse the very essence of his being: *awareness*. The focus of awareness has always been directed outward, on people, things, and events outside of self. The treasures of the outer world have been his only quest, but the paradox is, the kingdom has always been within!

I first came across the teachings of Vernon Howard almost twenty years ago. His book, *Psycho-Pictography*, seemed too practical and devoid of the "mystical" that so intrigued me then. Nevertheless, it struck a chord of truthfulness that I could never quite escape, and unknowingly I measured other teachers and philosophies by its practical standard.

After years of searching, trying, and discarding I was finally led back to Vernon Howard's first book, and others that he left behind. His was a true, methodical, almost scientific approach to developing "awareness." I regard his teachings as probably the only true western approach for achieving spiritual enlightenment and transformation. For those who are weary of the empty promises of the outward path and are ready for the less glamorous but no less rewarding path inward, these *lessons* will be your introduction to a new and higher world – the lost **Inner Kingdom**. This technology was inspired by Vernon Howard but contains the imprints of my own unique experience and viewpoints. I do not apologize for this personal tangent – all truth teachings adopt individual viewpoints – I only ask that you test these principles as presented and prove to yourself their rightness of source, then modify them to your own unique taste.

INTRODUCTION

This is a series of lessons forming a unique development course. There are two lessons to a "unit" and each unit contains two related lessons that compliment each other. Although these concepts are considered ancient wisdom, the lessons are fashioned after the more current works of Vernon Howard; his system was furthered by best-selling author Guy Finley; and the present work is updated and simplified by the author.

When you reach a certain level of awareness the world and the universe become a magical place. Things happen that would seem extraordinary to those less aware. Beautiful people walk up to you, look you in the eyes and send a tingle down your spine, they hand you a book, sometimes a simple written message, then disappear back into the crowd. No words need be spoken, but sometimes are. The information they leave and the impact of their presence leave a strong impression, and a profound influence. This may be in part telepathic.

All the materials you read here, in *The Super Awareness*, bear the imprint of this divine influence..."In the whole world only a few people are awake, and they live in a state of total, constant amazement!"

Chapter One: The False Self

Imagine a mechanical robot with an advanced electronic computer for a brain. As a mechanical being its movements are artificial, mere reflections of the smooth flowing patterns of human movement. Its brain, though an electronic marvel of sophisticated speed and memory storage capability, is still basically mechanical and artificial. This artificial man can only mimic the dynamic, fluid and spontaneous actions – both physical and mental -- of the real being who created it. Its life and expression are borrowed.

This artificial creation is very important to the understanding of who you are. Without realizing it you have created an artificial entity out of the stuff you are, given it a name, a whole personality, and sent it out to meet the world as your personal representative. I know this sounds bizarre and ridiculous ... but follow me along.

To fully understand this I have first to acquaint you with a psychological process that is so much a part of you, you don't even realize you use it. It is something so familiar you never question its reality or function. This mysterious process is called "Identification."

Have you ever wondered why movies captivate us so? For hours we can sit transfixed, unaware of our normal lives, living the adventure, romance, or chain of events of a fictional character on the screen. For those who like reading, a novel serves the same purpose. But here, a mysterious process is at work that is unique to human beings -- no other animal or living thing can possibly relate to this ability to project outside of itself and become something totally different than it is.

We have the unique capability of identifying with things and people outside us. To *identify with* is to fully relate to (in empathy with) another; to suspend reality and embrace the symbolic. Almost unaware we experience illusion as reality. Identification has so many different levels of expression, we don't even notice the shift from one to another. For instance, consider the word "lemon." It is just a word like any other, but what happens when we think of a real lemon? The "word" becomes empowered with smell and taste and this excites a host of automatic, involuntary reactions in the body. The taste buds in the mouth become activated, saliva begins to flow, and certain gastric juices in the stomach begin to stir. What has happened? Simply another facet of this process called Identification. We experienced an illusion as reality.

This is where the trouble begins. The process is so common, happening without conscious realization, and shifting so frequently, we identify more with illusions than we do with what is real.

Consider how little time you spend in the actual Present. Most of the time you're lost in thought -- either reliving the past through memory or anticipating the future by imagination. These unaware periods are other facets of Identification -- the mental movies we're running of the past or the future are still illusions that we project ourselves into. But we've missed the reality which is always in the Present, the here and now. And we've missed the reality of who we are as well.

In his book, *The Mystic Path To Cosmic Power*, Vernon Howard says:

"Identification means that we mentally or emotionally lose ourselves in something inside or outside of ourselves. We become absorbed in a person, a place, our career, a hobby, our personal viewpoints... When we identify with our thoughts, we call it daydreaming... Identification also means to wrongly take something as being part of our essential selves. Take your name. That is only a label attached at birth. If you change your name, it would not make *you* any different. Take the physical body. That is merely a vehicle for living on earth. Your True Self does not consist of name, body, money, home, career, or your personal beliefs. You are something entirely different from these attachments."

Is the light coming on? Can you see how illusion has replaced reality? Can you imagine the "you" that you've always identified with, may not be the real you after all?

- ❖ **The false self is a pretender** with many faces, and its main task is to keep you occupied with false pursuits that extend its illusory life. It is a creature that craves sensation (any and all) and its only life is the one you give it.

- ❖ **The false self has a mechanical, artificial nature.** It stores and retrieves memories like a computer. Its reactions are mechanical, having been learned and conditioned by past experience. It responds to all circumstances from habit.

- ❖ **It is the source of all doubt and anxiety**, of all negative thoughts, of all negative emotions, of all pain. The negative voices you hear whispering from within are always coming from the false self.

- ❖ **The false self is master of pretense and lies.** It not only lies to others, but to itself as well. A master of disguise, it pretends to be anything to anyone. Its many voices continually change, disguising itself in myriad roles.

- ❖ **It is always focused outward to the world of possessions,** things and activities that enhance only its own self-interests and flattered image. It seeks the constant approval of others to validate its slowly eroding façade.

- ❖ **It is only focused in the past or the future.** That's why it keeps your mind running from the pleasures and self-flattering images of the past to the hopeful dreams of accomplishment in the future. It also torments you with the failures of the past, and the anxieties of the future.

Does this creature sound familiar? It should, because you know it intimately. It has stolen your real life and given you nothing but despair and uncertainty in return. Its hidden name is [Ego].

The following stories and illustrations will give you a sense of the false self and its activities. You will recognize the emerging true self as it tries to re-awaken from the confusion of its illusions.

One other note. Vernon Howard said stories and illustrations are used as tools to entice the mind to accept *Truth* teachings. Otherwise, the false self might cause us to forget. He called these stories "Psycho-Pictograms" because they had a way of lodging themselves in the subconscious, acting just below the surface and reminding us of the proper ways to respond to Reality. Philosophers and adepts from ages past have used the power pictures, planted by way of stories, to enhance their student's memory and serve as subconscious guidelines. I do the same here, however using an updated term: Subliminal Pictograph.

***

THE TRICKSTER

There was once a smart old crow who lived by himself in a vast forest. Because of his devious and deceitful ways, he had long ago been banished from the crow community. The other animals in the forest knew him well and for the most part kept their distance when he was around. He had deceived many unsuspecting critters in the past with stories of his magical powers and promises of good fortune to those who carried out his wishes. But time and again his promises had failed and the only good fortune that came, came only to the crow, after taking advantage of the good will and hard work of others.

One day he came across a baby eaglet that had fallen from its nest, left abandoned. Always one to seize an opportunity, the old crow saw devious advantage in taking the orphan and raising it as his own.

The baby eagle soon forgot its majestic parent, and through a process of identification peculiar to birds, it imprinted itself to the identity of the crow. Thinking the crow was its parent, it mimicked the crow in every way. The eaglet tried and tried but always failed to please the crow, for the cunning trickster knew well the psychology of deceit; he had his own plans for the trusting infant.

As time went on the eaglet grew larger and stronger than his adopted parent. But by now the crow had shackled him with heavy mental chains -- chains that kept his budding strength in check while curbing a natural curiosity for the open spaces. Warnings to never venture beyond a certain boundary were strictly reinforced; to disobey was to be cursed. His criticism of the eaglet was unceasing ... he was too big, too ugly, and too awkward. The crow also knew that an eagle needed meat to grow to its potential, so he kept his captive on a strict diet of grain. Corn grain was plentiful in an adjacent farmer's field, so the little eagle became too fat to fly very high or very far…but he was still very strong.

Now the crow had a faithful servant to do his work, and do his bidding. The other critters in the forest had watched with alarm as the eagle grew, not knowing what evil intent the crow might have. But soon they would see...

The old crow was a creature who thrived on power and possessions, but he understood that other creatures were necessary to satisfy his needs. No one could be an island to himself, and no one could be a king *by* himself. Or so he believed. His plan then, was to rule the woodlands and keep for himself the treasures of his fellow creatures.

Cunningly he persuaded the eagle orphan to extend their territory by bullying the other critters ... to abandon their homes, nests, and burrows, to leave behind their treasures and stockpiled goods ... unless of course they agreed to work for the crow and build his kingdom.

The eagle had a gentle nature and he knew inside that what he was doing violated some innate law. It just didn't feel right! But he was obligated to the crow, the only authority he'd ever known ... and it was curious (if not satisfying) to see the power he had over others. His mere presence it seemed was enough to make other critters cower and feign his favor. So with reluctance he used his powers of persuasion, and when necessary direct force to evict others and expand the crow's territory.

The territory grew and the kingdom made its profits. But reality has a way of resisting *falseness* and restoring the *true*. The little eagle became discouraged. Despite his position and power, he felt alone and out of place. He had somehow become separated from Nature, from the wholeness he'd felt part of as a youngster. He had become a bully and a liar ... but his mentor the crow was finally praising him. He was doing the right thing and making them both rich. But if it was right, why did it feel so wrong?

THE DAWNING OF AWARENESS HAD COME...

The small voice of reason within kept asking him that same question over and over again, each and every day. Each time he violated this (seeming unseen law) the inner voice made him aware and made him feel the disharmony of his act.

AWARENESS ITSELF HOLDS THE POWER TO CHANGE, TO TRANSFORM...

Each violation was swiftly followed by a reaction of Awareness. Ten times, twenty times, and more... until he could no longer tolerate the conflict within. Finally the little eagle made a momentous decision: he would leave the kingdom to escape the tyranny of his mentor, and leave behind the comforts of the only home he'd ever known.

THE CHALLENGE OF AWARENESS IS TO LEAVE FALSENESS BEHIND...

(story continued later...)

***

SUBLIMINAL PICTOGRAPHS

THE GREAT ILLUSIONIST

Harry Houdini was considered the greatest magician who ever lived. His illusions not only surprised and astounded his adoring public, but they aroused the most intense feelings of identification that common men could imagine. Each time he struggled with chains and defied death by fire, water or earth, those who watched experienced sympathetic agony. After long moments of tortured waiting ... came the relief of glorious escape. Symbolically his feats of escape lifted men to uncommon heights of freedom, then ultimate relief.

But Houdini by his own admission was never quite satisfied. The real "escape" he sought was always out of reach. The hunger to become ever bigger and better drove him to constantly re-invent himself, and his death defying acts, again and again. For all his fame, money, mystique and public adoration, Houdini never found the "ultimate peace that satisfies all hungers."

Houdini did not die in the water torture escape, as was widely believed, but of a ruptured appendix. One day he proudly challenged a young man to "give his best shot" to the stomach. Houdini fancied himself a man of steel ... his boastful challenges were only a vain attempt to bolster a fleeting self-image. But alas he had met his match, and the point where a man's pride must meet the test of reality proved fatal.

Houdini, the man of steel, lingered for a week on his deathbed. During periods of lucidity, when only drugs relieved his agony, he became friends with the attending physician. He soon confided, "You know Doctor, before all this began I once considered becoming a doctor myself. What a fulfilling life it would have been -- relieving pain and suffering, curing sickness and making people whole again..."

"But Mr. Houdini," the doctor countered, "with all your success, fame and adoration, how could you possibly have fancied a different life?"

"Because what you do is *real*." He sighed and looked into the doctor's eyes. "My whole life has been a *fake*!"

***

A COUNTERFEIT BLESSING

The cuckoo bird is a con artist, known as the parasite of the bird kingdom. Each spring when other birds have made their nests and laid their eggs, the mature cuckoo waits for an opportunity to deposit its eggs into the nest of another species. When the parents are away looking for food, the cuckoo secrets its own egg into the nest and flies away without care or regret. The unsuspecting parents return and never notice the new egg, and never question its authenticity. As they warm and care for the eggs, nothing seems unusual ... until the chicks are born. Then oddly one of the new arrivals is big, and uncommonly loud. Its needs and appetite far exceed that of the others and its constant pleas for food keep the parents in a busy frenzy. They rush through each day hypnotized by the cries of their false offspring. The cuckoo grows very fast in size and strength and soon it rids the nest of its weaker siblings. They're simply nudged out and left for prey. The parents meanwhile expend all their energies and attention on the big, loud, complaining counterfeit. He grows bigger than his adopted parents -- and soon they become so exhausted they can no longer supply the needed nourishment. The cuckoo then reluctantly leaves the nest.

Chapter Two: The True Self

The *True Self* is indescribable. Words and concepts and metaphors can only hint at its reality and possibilities. It is like the eye that looks out upon the world, but never sees itself. The real self can see and function *in* the world, but it cannot fully comprehend itself, other than to know it *Is*. And don't confuse this with the "airy" and ambiguous descriptions of soul and higher self. It is *you*, here and now. It is not some future perfect being, barely connected with you as you know yourself to be. It may *have* soul and it may *be* the higher self, but whatever it is, it is your very life and being.

Perhaps the best definition of the real self would be, simply: ***aware will***. It is a point of awareness and volition in a sea of consciousness. This definition at least describes its highest function, as we will show later.

Imagine a majestic lighthouse sitting on a point of land overlooking the ocean. The light-house itself is physical (like the physical body) but at the very top resides a magical property unlike anything physical: a bright light! The light itself has very unusual properties. Its speed is the fastest thing known to physical science; its particles can act either as individual units, or blend into huge waves or patterns (gestalts). The light from a lighthouse can be pointed in any direction ... its beam focused to the narrow intensity of a laser, or diffused to a wide spectrum. Consciousness can be likened to light.

Though the lighthouse may be consumed by fog, rain, snow, storms, and high winds, the light travels out with no restraint -- unimpeded by the forces of nature or the ravages of time. The true self too is unaffected by the passing storms of our lives. Its nature is something quite apart from the things we experience, or the notions we entertain.

This is but one small piece of the puzzle of our true nature. To re-emphasize, words and concepts and metaphors only hint at the reality of this unknown part of ourselves.

However, a tried and true method handed down by philosophers and scientists of old may best serve our quest for this elusive self. It states: "To deduce the nature of something not known, eliminate all that it is *not*." Do you remember the multiple choice quiz from high school? You may not have known the correct answer to a question, but by eliminating all the choices you knew were wrong, you could logically assume that what was left was right. Then there was the true or false quiz. If you knew which was false ... the other then was true.

Since the false self is false, let us begin there. By knowing the false, we can assume its opposite is probably true, or at least a closer approximation.

- ❖ If the false self is a pretender with many faces, the real self must be the true reflection of you. It is your most basic and indivisible aspect -- your essence or individual self.

- ❖ If the false self has a mechanical artificial nature, then the real self must be spontaneous, natural, and pure. Without the complexity of diverse parts it is essentially simple and uncomplicated.

- ❖ If the false self is the source of anxiety, doubt, and pain, of negative thought and emotion, then the real self must be a wellspring of calmness and contentment, of positive energy, a silent voice of encouragement within.

- ❖ If the false self is master of pretense and lies, then the real self is our connection to Truth, Reality, God.

- ❖ If the false self focuses attention and energy outward ... if it needs the constant approval of others, then the real self is independent and whole, its reality is self-contained (but connected with All That Is).

- ❖ If the false self is only focused in the past or the future, the real self-resides in the Now.

These deductions at least give a clue to the information we're seeking. A further unraveling by a method known as "detachment deduction" will get us even closer to an experiential awareness of our true self.

Let's begin with the most intimate object we identify with: the physical body. Most people think the body is the whole self, that it contains all the person is: his personality and IQ, all beliefs, desires, habits and skills.

They think that without the body there is no *being*. Of course those who are religious *believe* there is something more, but belief is not experience so they really do not *know*. But the body is, in reality, only a vehicle for the expression of the **self**. Like the automobile - something we also identify with - it is only a tool with a useful purpose.

Since we are using logic to unveil useful information, let me begin with a useful axiom: "Anything we attach ourselves to, *by identification*, is separate from our real self … it is either a useful tool, or an attached illusion."

Look at your hand. Will it to move as you wish. Can you see and feel that it is a mechanical expression (though wondrously so) of your conscious will? Choose any other part of the body. Does it not function likewise? Your entire body functions like a useful tool, under the guidance of a superior aspect: the conscious will.

We can deduce therefore that whatever the self may or may not be, it is <u>not</u> the body. The body is a tool, a vehicle -- not the operator.

Another useful axiom is: "Anything that *changes* can be considered a *dimensional* property and therefore not the true self." For the sake of simplicity we'll call all things subject to the laws of change "dimensional," and conversely all things not subject to change "non-dimensional." The body in the above illustration *changes* daily and also by stages: from infant, to childhood, to teen, to adult, to senior. It is therefore *dimensional*.

❖ The true self resides outside of dimensions and can be considered non-dimensional essence; it has the stable (unchanging) characteristics of consistency and constancy.

The next (higher) aspect we identify with is feelings, the emotional nature. When you say, "I am happy" or "I am sad," you identify with the feelings of happiness or sadness. These (or any other) feelings are not you. They are simply *useful functions* of expression, or tools of expression if you like.

Can you not step back, like an observer or a witness, and simply behold your emotion as it rises ... then falls? As a detached observer you can see that you have *identified* with some-thing not you, and you can also see that feelings and emotions *change*. These exclude the emotions from being the real you.

We can deduce therefore that whatever the self may or may not be, it is not the emotions. The emotions are useful functions of expression -- not the being who expresses the emotion.

The next (higher) aspect we identify with is the mind, the mental nature. This includes our individual IQ and mental aptitudes, our thoughts and beliefs, even concepts about ourselves that make up our personalities. When you are seemingly *lost in thought*, can you see that you are identified with those thoughts, that they seem to be you? Can you see that the beliefs you hold are merely mental concepts, things inside that you've mis-identified as being you? These mental constructs (or any others) are not you. They are simply *useful functions* of mental expression, they give the means of separating things into understandable qualities. It is the nature of thought to separate and classify, but thought is not you.

Can you not step back, like an observer or a witness, and simply behold your thoughts as they come and go? As a detached observer, you can see that you've *identified* with something not you, and you can also see that thoughts and beliefs *change*. These exclude the mind from being the real you.

We can deduce therefore that whatever the self may or may not be, it is not thought, mind, or any of its constructs. Thought is a useful function, a tool for constructing and making sense of the world – but it is not the being who expresses it.

And now we cross a great divide, into a dimension much closer to the real self, but still not quite there. Most of what we have "detached" from so far would seem far enough for most people ... but if we would persist in our quest there is yet more to uncover. Here now is the realm of ***aware-will***.

The ***will*** is an aspect of our true being, without it there would be no outer thrust or forward movement. All would be as calm as a sea, without life, movement or direction. The will is at the core of our being and of infinite importance to our life and well-being. It is, even so, a tool of *useful function* and subject to the law of *change*. It is not our real being.

Can you not step back, like an observer or a witness, and behold the will as it functions to greater or lesser degree? As a detached observer, you can see that you've *identified* with something not you, and you can also see that it *changes*. These exclude the will from being the real you.

Awareness is an aspect of our true being, without it there would be no realization. All would be calm as a sea, without *realization* that it even exists. Awareness is at the very core of our being, and necessary to the realization that we are ***being***. It is, even so, subject to change. The awareness can be focused like a laser or it can be radiated like the light of the sun.

Can you not step back, like an observer or a witness, and behold awareness as it functions through a spectrum: from focused to radiating? As a detached observer, you can see that it *changes*.

And so we can deduce, that whatever the real self may or may not be, it is not the ***will*** or the ***awareness***. These are at the very core of its being, but are still only aspects of what ***it** is*.

To cross the next divide and go beyond the known dimensions, is to step into the realm of the real self. It is the true "unknown," a region of purity and constancy that can hardly be described or imagined. As the source of all *manifested* dimensions, it is itself *un-manifest* and *non-dimensional*. Physicists call this realm The Quantum Field. It is timeless and formless, pervading all space and time, it is the source of all power and energy in whatever form, it is the *base stuff* that connects All things as One thing. It is both intelligent and nurturing; it is constant and changeless.

In bringing it all back to a more personal level, how can we best relate to this mysterious, infinite, powerful aspect of who we are? The best we can do (in words at least) is to describe it as ultimate ***self-consciousness***, the ultimate **witness** of all we feel and experience. The Quantum is live, ***pure consciousness***, and our own defining piece of this infinite substance is our own self-consciousness. We're a mere bubble in a sea of awareness. There is nothing more to say, except maybe, it is the ***"I Am."***

Although we have *detached* from these useful

functions and aspects of ourselves, this in no way diminishes their importance to our lives. They are as much a part of us as our "humanness" and cannot be denied their useful expression. Our purpose in this exercise was to arrive at an understanding of our real being, aside from that which changes and is considered part of the manifest "dimensional" universe.

Now you may ask, "Why do these tools or expressions of ourselves ... the body, the mind, the emotions ... sometimes get out of control and seem to act as though they have a will of their own? For example: physical illness, mental illness, runaway thoughts and emotions. In other words, why do these useful tools and functions turn against us?"

The answer is simple, and something you must make yourself aware of each time it happens. It is the *false self*. You have delegated control to the false aspect of yourself, allowing *it* to use these tools for its own purposes. If you can make yourself "aware" each time it happens, you will gradually break the "spell" of the false self and wrestle back the power you have unconsciously given away. The false self after all is just a tool itself, but because of our own mental laziness, it has become our master ... instead of our servant.

***

(story continued...)

The little eagle was determined to leave behind the past and search out a more meaningful life ... whatever, or wherever that may be. At first, he thought of confronting the crow and then just leaving, but he knew the persuasiveness of his elder. So instead, he stole away into a starlit night while the trickster slept.

At first he felt dazed and confused. The trickster's words, like old tapes, played relentless in his head. Fears welled to the surface. He came to the boundary of his previous world, the ring-pass-not, but another voice, softer and deeper within, urged him on in spite of the fear and confusion. Pressing through the invisible ring, a remarkable thing happened...

The fear and trembling faded away. A heavy weight within seemed to disintegrate. He felt a lightness and freedom like he'd never known. Now he could begin the quest without looking back.

FACING A FEAR WITH AWARENESS, DISSOLVES IT FOREVER...

For several days he wandered, searching for some clue that might unlock the secret of his past and provide the key to his quest. The forest was alive with sights and sounds that he had never encountered before, but he stayed alert and maintained his calm.

Then he heard something. Somewhere in the distance two birds chattered back and forth, one to the other. The sound was strange, a gobble-gobble-gobble, but nevertheless a birdlike sound. He followed it to a small clearing and there found two dark-feathered creatures with fanned tail plumage. These birds were unlike any he'd ever seen.

He approached slowly, being careful not to startle them, and asked if they might chat a while. They agreed in a friendly manner, and he began to explain himself. Soon they were friends.

The little eagle was invited to dinner. This would give him a chance to learn more about them and their customs. The others he met were also very friendly, chatting openly about themselves and their beliefs. Everyone seemed fond of the eagle and one thing led to another. Soon he was asked to stay. He secretly wondered if this was home, if these were his kin, and so he agreed.

The gobblers, as he called them, admired his strength. All the tedious, heavy-lifting jobs were saved for him alone. Although they were courteous, he could tell they regarded him as only a menial worker of somewhat lower status. They grew lazy, and he grew resentful. As before, he never seemed to quite fit in with the others. Always the odd one, he still felt alone and unappreciated for who he was inside. Besides, the constant chatter of these gobblers gave him a headache. So as before he stole away into the night. No good-bye, and no regrets.

AWARENESS OF THE FALSE OPENS THE WAY TO THE TRUE...

Long days passed as he ventured deeper into the woods. The grain meal he was used to became nonexistent and soon he was forced to find other nourishment. The few berries, nuts, and acorns he managed to find were hardly satisfying ... something inside urged a change, to find new foods.

He heard a rustling of leaves and the flapping of wings. Investigating, he found another strange bird devouring the remains of a rabbit. This bird was large and black, his beak looked sharp and lethal, it was ideal for tearing flesh. The bird seemed startled and defensive when the little eagle stepped out of the brush. "Don't worry," the eagle assured, "I am no threat, and I certainly have no desire for your meal."

The new creature changed posture, straightening his legs and back. Now he was taller than the eagle, inspecting his adversary with a piercing glare. "Why should I believe that?" he challenged the newcomer, "This critter has the sweetest meat of any."

"I don't eat flesh!" the eagle proclaimed, "What a strange food." He was shocked at the notion.

The bird relaxed and returned to the eagle's eye level. "Well then, perhaps you should try it sometime. You seem a bit unusual for one of your kind."

"There are others like me?" he blurted, excited at the possibility. "I've been searching for my home, my kin. Could you tell me where they live?"

"Oh, I seldom see them. They fly higher and farther than the rest of us. I suspect they live in the high country, over the horizon."

"But I can't fly very far," the eagle confided. "Only fifty yards at a time, at most, like the gobblers in the pine forest."

"Oh, I see," the vulture said with sympathy. "Perhaps it's your diet. I know that **eagles** eat meat. Maybe if you tried it, you'd be able to fly like them."

"**Eagles** ... is that what they're called? is that what I am?"

The eagle and the vulture became friends. Soon the little eagle was able to eat meat ... he filled out quickly and his wings developed full strength. And with a little help from the vulture, he also learned to fly high and far like real eagles do.

To fly was to be free. The potential had always been there, awaiting the right circumstances to be released. And as he looked down from thousands of feet in the sky, his eyes were new, he saw a realm like he'd never dreamed. The trees, the rivers, the creatures below, all existed for his enjoyment. A more lofty life, he could not imagine. This was what he was meant to find. He was content. In time, he found others like himself … and new adventures to share with those, who like him, had eyes to see.

Chapter Three: The Witness

By now you should have at least a "sense" of what you are, and what you are not. This does not mean that the false self is non-existent. It is still valid because you created it. But whatever you create, you can also un-create. This requires an almost magical act however; it is a secret that only adepts have known and used.

There is something you must first understand. Evolution and the enlightenment of the human mind requires letting go of the old, not adding something new. We're normally taught to go after and actively pursue what we desire. To seek out and acquire more. Self-improvement, too, implies adding something to what we lack. This mind-set has led us down a road that can never lead to real, lasting contentment. No sooner do we achieve what we had sought, when another want or desire manifests and drives us to yet another desire. It seems we can never rest for long in the satisfaction of what we've achieved. The merry-go-round of life keeps turning ... on and on we go, constantly in pursuit of that elusive something, but rarely enjoying.

This is how the theme of our website, Super Awareness, serves as a reminder of what we must do. The real treasures of life are revealed only as we empty ourselves of the useless baubles we've acquired. What are these baubles? They can be anything (physical, emotional, or mental) that weigh us down and hold us back. For example: that high priced car that flatters the ego but wastes the wallet; that relationship that seemed so good but now is so draining; the opinion or belief that seemed so right and gave us stability, now has so many holes that we're constantly patching it up or trying to defend it.

We refuse to part with these burdens because:
1. they seem so familiar
2. we worked hard to get them, and
3. without them there would be a void.

All of these reasons, I assure you, are only rationalizations of the false self. What we need to do is "detach" from these false treasures, accepting with awareness the uncomfortable void, then allowing the **true** (for you) to fill the void and take its place.

But to prove to you the validity of the above, just reflect on how good it feels to finally decide, then remove, what has been weighing you down. How good does it feel to clear the clutter of "stuff" from the garage or attic? How good does it feel to end a faulty relationship and move on? How good does it feel when you drop a frozen attitude like, "I have to do what others want, regardless of what I want, to keep their approval."

***

THE HOT AIR BALLOON

Imagine a brightly colored hot air balloon sitting on the desert sand, alone and unattended. You've been lost in the desert for days; you're thirsty and hungry and on the verge of collapse. You spot this bright colored sphere from a distance and wonder if it's just a mirage. As you get closer your mind makes a hundred excuses for why it shouldn't be there. But you press on. Finally arriving, your senses are filled with its undeniable reality and you feel the thrill of possible rescue... But no one is inside. You have no idea how to fly a balloon. Again your mind turns negative and warns you of the dangers of such a contraption. But you ignore its warnings and climb aboard. After minutes of exploring the contraption, an idea occurs to you. Just drop the useless sandbags. As you untie the heavy bags they drop to the ground and the balloon lifts off. The dreadful heat disappears as you go higher, leaving behind the desert and the dangers of its reality. Rescue is assured.

Spiritual enlightenment is more a matter of discard than attainment...

Now to reveal a secret process that has been used for ages to achieve true enlightenment. It is only one of a handful of real secrets you'll ever need. Therefore keep it to yourself ... keep it always in mind ... and keep it growing with continued practice.

As you have learned, one of the purest aspects of our true nature is awareness. You have heard the term many times, but do you really know what it is? Simply -- it is life itself! Without awareness and sensation you'd only be a lump of clay, living perhaps, but not alive. Awareness can be focused, like the rays of the sun through a magnifying glass ... we call this alertness or attention. It can also be diffuse and unfocused, like a candle radiating its light all around ... we call this passive-awareness, or just being conscious. But who decides the degree of awareness brought to bear on any situation? You do. And how do you do that? By exercising your will. Again we see the close relationship between awareness and will. These are the basic ingredients, the essence, of You.

Awareness is passive; will is active. Like all things (that are really one thing) there is a positive side and a negative side. Negative does not mean bad, it's just the polar opposite of positive, like a battery with positive and negative poles.

If you've followed along this far, and you understand what I've tried to relate with mere words, you now have the basis for understanding the secret...

Behind all things you experience in life is the Invisible Witness. It is a projection of the true self, always present, witnessing all that happens – and witnessing your reactions to all that happens. It is really you, but the part of you you've always ignored because you've been erroneously identified with the false self. Our task is to detach from (discard) the false self, and reclaim the lost powers, abilities, and innate contentment of the true self. To do this however requires an almost magical process ... which we call upon the Invisible Witness to help us achieve.

To identify with the Witness is to capture the essence of Awareness. It sees all but judges nothing. Remember this: It sees all, but judges nothing. This is a knack that will take some time to cultivate, because we've been conditioned to judge everything. From childhood to present we've been taught to classify all things as either good or bad, right or wrong, fair or unfair … black or white. By being on one side, we must do constant battle with its opposite. This has created an imbalance in our lives, which is not natural. But more on this later.

Let's try an experiment to catch a glimpse of the Witness. Stop all thought, take a step back (away from yourself), and just observe. Where are you and what are you doing at this very moment? Watch yourself looking into the monitor, or reading this page. To use an old phrase: Can you not step back, like an observer or a witness, and simply behold yourself doing what you're doing? Ask yourself this question: Where are you, and what are you doing?

Take a moment…

OK. Did you feel a different level of awareness? Did you capture the feeling of being fully centered in the moment?

Try it again…

As the Witness you play the part of a scientist, you observe with detachment what you are looking at. There is no judgment, only curiosity. What you see is not good or bad, it simply Is.

This is the attitude you want to cultivate. Try to catch the feeling of this non-judging witness, as many times in your day as you can. It will take time, so go easy on yourself … don't even judge your progress. Understand, the way you normally experience everyday life is similar to a state of hypnosis. Your mind has been conditioned to see things from only one viewpoint, and that one viewpoint influences <u>everything</u> in your life. What we want to do is snap the spell of your hypnosis by "waking up" many times each day. With practice you will be able to hold that waking moment longer and longer. Then you will at least have an alternative viewpoint, and an alternative level of consciousness to work from. I cannot promise that you'll be able to hold that state all day long; it's not necessary. Since we live in this world, we must function in this world with its customary state of consciousness. Otherwise, we might seem strange to others. But also, there appears to be a frequency barrier of some sort that surrounds our earth and keeps the activity of our brains confined to certain parameters. Why it is, and who put it there, I cannot say. I only know that it resists the "waking state" that we want to achieve.

The Witness remember is unconditioned, pure awareness; and it sometimes needs the assistance of its active ally, the will. You will need the will, not only to steer the awareness, but also to hold its focus on what you're observing. In the beginning it will tend to wander, like the curiosity of a small child. Realize that this is only natural and not to be scorned. Simply lead it back and re-focus. This is much like meditation, and in fact it probably is. However instead of sitting cross-legged, breathing slowly, concentrating on something, you will be using the raw material of everyday circumstance to center yourself and wake up. We might call this "waking meditation." Keep in mind the objective: We want to detach from the illusory life of the false self, and re-identify with our real self and the real life we were meant to enjoy. To do this we must shake the semi-hypnosis of normal consciousness and re-awaken the aware state of real consciousness. The training of the Witness is key.

Do not assume this is a pie-in-the-sky idealistic philosophy that sounds good but does not work. This is a practical, workable process that changes simple observations into meaningful realizations, and leads to higher and higher levels of awareness. It is progress you can see and feel. However, you must work with patience and perseverance. If you can convince yourself that this is the most important work in your life – that nothing, no matter what, will grant you more enduring rewards – you will then have the proper attitude to succeed. And besides, you are using the everyday material of your own life to progress. Imagine, your own life is your best teacher! Now that's natural ... that's the way it was supposed to be.

***

CLIMBING THE MOUNTAIN

This is a Vernon Howard story. During a battle of the Middle Ages, a king's life was saved by an archer in the ranks. In gratitude, the king declared to the soldier, "Climb up the mountain trail for a period of six hours. All the land that is viewed from the top-most height shall be yours. The higher you ascend the more you possess."

The archer hiked upward, pausing at intervals to rest. At each halt, the king's officers gazed across the countryside, making note of the most distant landmark. The higher the soldier climbed, the more territory the king's men claimed for him. Finally, the soldier possessed a vast area of land with all its natural wealth.

Acting on the king's promise, the soldier became more wealthy the higher he climbed. By steadily uplifting your own level of awareness, you too will be rich. You will attract advantages in more variety than you can imagine. Try to see that there are many different levels of awareness and understanding. Also see that the higher your awareness, the more you attract the genuinely good things of life.

There is one other characteristic of awareness that you should understand before we proceed. It is the ability of awareness to dissolve and remove unwanted conditions and circumstances. We might call this uncreating what we have no further use for. It is also used in conjunction with detachment and discard, the two properties we've been discussing thus far.

Let's try another experiment. As you sit here reading, there is probably something in your body that's signaling for attention. It can be anything, like mild anxiety, lingering anger with a friend or family member, a minor ache or pain, any annoyance. You've become quite adept at tuning out these minor irritations, leaving them to fester beneath consciousness, not knowing that left "unprocessed" they steal your energy, rob your health, and ultimately block your spiritual progress. To consciously treat these irritations is to "process" them. Here's how:

Turn the force of your attention to one of these

nagging signals. Suppose for instance you focus upon the anxiety you feel in the pit of your stomach. You realize it has been there for quite awhile, days even, gnawing at your insides like a rat in an apple crate. But somehow you've managed to ignore or suppress it, for just as long. No longer! From now on you're going to tune in to these annoyances and eliminate them one by one ... as soon as they first occur. How? With awareness.

First, try to locate the exact place in your body where this annoyance is occurring. In our example, anxiety, it is probably in the pit of your stomach (although it could also be anywhere between the intestines and the heart). Now bring your full awareness to that area. Try to define the boundary or perimeter of discomfort. Use your imagination and color this area with a drab gray or a dull brown. If the area changes shape, follow it and color it again with your imagination. Just keep steady attention focused there. Also <u>feel</u> the feeling. Try to define it. Is it a dull discomfort? a throbbing or an aching pain? an empty void? Whatever the feeling, feel it fully. If your mind (or the false self) tries to distract you, bring your full attention back, again and again, if necessary. Soon you will notice the discomfort fading away. The annoyance has just been processed, and instead of merely treating the symptom you have taken a chunk out of the cause. Each time it presents itself to consciousness -- from now on – you will steer your full awareness there and bring your focus on it again. With time, you will eliminate the problem altogether. This is the power of awareness...

Chapter Four: Self-Observation

The *Witness*, of course, is used for self-observation. However, this process is much more involved than mere words like *self-observing* can relate. You will have to question "why" to practically everything you previously <u>did</u> without question. The realm of self-honesty is pivotal here, so you must try to uncover <u>why</u> you do what you do. You will be surprised with the many rationalizations you use to give a good face to otherwise questionable activities. You will be annoyed at the many contradictions you have allowed to exist between your thoughts and your actions, between the facts and your beliefs. In short, you will be disappointed to find all the ways you have lied to yourself.

These are not to be used as judgment against yourself though. This is a whole new game. No longer will you judge yourself, and others, then fester inside. Instead you will observe without criticism what you do, then ask yourself <u>*why*</u> you did it. You want to investigate and uncover your intentions – your real intentions. And as you do this, I promise, your awareness will step in with its own magic and clear away the debris of all these self-contradictions. Then you will know the feeling of innocence again. And innocence is the state of being of your true self.

So let's start with the process of self-honesty. If you could step back and view yourself from the standpoint of the Witness, which you can, you would be amazed at all the crazy inconsistencies and contradictions you allow within yourself. Take any circumstance that comes into your life. They are all gifts, by the way, that you've attracted to teach you, about you. Suppose for example a friend comes to you and asks a favor. In your mind you have built a self-image of being the *loyal and helpful friend*, giving of yourself whenever asked, no matter the inconvenience to your own life. Now your friend, knowing this, can and frequently does take advantage of this weakness (but because of your upbringing and Christian faith, you think it's a strength). The friend has a little boy and she needs you to baby sit for the evening. She has a date with a new suitor. Her little boy is quite precocious and always into some sort of mischief. You really hate to watch him, but of course you agree to. And you have a terrible evening. Your friend doesn't make it back home that evening, she doesn't even call, and you have to keep the little imp all night long. Next morning she shows up, apologizes, and goes her way with barely a thank you. "Oh well," you say to yourself, "God is watching and I know he'll be impressed with my good deed."

Get a grip, Woman! First, there is no wise old white-haired bearded God sitting in Heaven, checking off merits and demerits with a pad and pencil. Of course today he probably uses a laptop computer. Second, how do you rationalize that anything good can come from a night of anxiety and inconvenience to you?

Now let's suppose that her dawning awareness, after years of suffering, has forced her to a realization ... she sees the futility of trying to please others. Then by coincidence, she reads something in a ladies magazine that brings it all home. It asks in so many words, "Would a rational person consciously hurt herself?" Her answer of course is <u>no</u>! So she reflects...

Her whole life, she finds, has been a repeating role ... of subservience to others. Few times had she put her own needs and desires first; and few times had her good deeds ever benefited her. Was that rational? she asked. Had she been consciously hurting herself ...with anxiety, inconvenience, and resentment? These negative emotions were punishment in themselves. So was it rational to put other people first?

This is an example of how awareness, when activated, can change your viewpoint. But there are still other issues that need to be addressed before lasting change, and a step to the next level of awareness can be realized.

As so often happens after a brief awakening, the means to higher revelations appear, almost magically...

Suppose she browses the bookstore and finds a book you're now reading. "That example sure sounds like me," she muses. She reads on, amused at the coincidence.

I have <u>these</u> comments for the lady in the preceding

example: "Your first mistake was in trying to maintain a faulty self-image. The image of a loyal, helpful, giving friend, giving of herself till it hurts. OK, that's an admirable image, a good Christian image, but wake up! Ask yourself: Have I really ever benefited from all my good deeds? Don't rationalize now, and don't mentally shift to "my good deeds will be rewarded eventually." Sure, you may have felt good for a few fleeting moments, but it never lasted. What we're after here is a feeling of contentment that lasts <u>always</u>. Those fleeting moments of feeling good were enticements from the false self to keep you on the merry-go-round. Soon you'd be out looking for another fix. Someone else to help. It goes on and on. Look lady, once you go back to your true self, you're led to heroic acts by inspiration alone, and everything feels good all the time."

But let's return to self-image ... it is a many faceted mirror of the false self. It reflects a different image [a mechanical image] to each situation and person it encounters. Remember that these [images] are conditioned, habitual responses learned and stored in memory from years of practice, *mechanical* therefore. But "image" is not real anyway. It's only a complex thought that masquerades as you, from somewhere in your memory. It is not you. It *is* what you've identified with though. So from now on try to connect the words *image* and *illusion*. They are both the same.

Now let's talk about the contradictions you allow, that share the same space within you. To be whole, to be true, there must be a continuity from <u>Thought</u> --> <u>Feeling</u> --> <u>Word</u> --> <u>Deed</u>. There is a natural order here, from the innermost to the outermost, and it must flow evenly. If there is just one contradiction to that even flow, from inside to outside, a blockage occurs and a suppression (suppressed expression) is added to the subconscious. All suppressions of like kind are stored in the same relative place, and they keep building. At some time they become powerful enough to manifest. The subconscious is indeed quite powerful, and eventually it will manifest a suppressed expression outward. This can take the form of an illness, as symptoms of pain or depression, or it (the subconscious) may directly attract an outside circumstance that forces you to deal with the subject of that particular suppression. Sooner or later Reality has a way of restoring the True, with lessons that are hard to ignore. You then have a choice: It can be done the easy way (by awareness and processing), or it can be done the hard way (if you keep resisting).

The lady in our example, after years of suffering the ill effects of her particular blockage, had finally had enough. She allowed the light of awareness to intervene and do its good work for her. But do you see the contradictions, from inner to outer, that she allowed in the first place? Whenever someone took advantage of her, her thought would say no! ... her feelings would say no! ... her words would say yes ... and her actions were also yes. Do you see the self-contradiction taking place here? If you do, be on the lookout for it in yourself.

Self-observation is the key. Be ready to detach from your normal consciousness and jump into the Witness. That simple act not only changes your level of awareness, it also provides a way to change a persistent problem.

***

THE ICEBERG

Imagine you're on a boat and you've been weathering storms and high seas for months. Your home port is finally in sight. But blocking the entrance to the channel that will take you all the way home is a gigantic iceberg. Everyone knows that what you see of an iceberg on the surface is only one tenth of its mass. The rest is hidden below. How do you get around it?

You can't get around it. It's stuck in the channel and no one can get in, or out. The problem seems insurmountable and will take a supernormal effort to solve.

During your travels you met a stranger at sea. He had no water or food but offered to trade a strange contraption he'd found on a deserted island. He said it had magical powers. You felt sorry for the stranger and would have shared your food and water anyway, but he insisted you take the artifact in trade. Reluctantly you accepted the gift – it was a metal rod with a crystal on one end and a box-like array at the other – and you stowed it below.

An idea occurs. Maybe that strange artifact could help. After bringing it topside you take a closer look. You are simply mystified with what it is, and how it works ... but you point it at the iceberg, hoping in imagination that it will somehow break up that huge chunk of ice. Whap!

The artifact discharges like a laser-gun and knocks the top off the iceberg. The berg rises to compensate and seems to grow more. Again you imagine a discharge. Whap! It blows more chunks off the berg. It rises again. Each discharge seems stronger and disintegrates larger and larger chunks of ice ... until at last only a field of floating ice chips remain. The way home is clear.

Like that strange artifact, you too have an almost magical weapon stowed below awaiting your use. Your awareness, directed by will and imagination, will disintegrate those blockages you've ignored for so long. But now, instead of ignoring these, you will focus your awareness on them as soon as they appear. Bit by bit the whole blockage will be dissolved and you'll have that much less "baggage" to haul around. But remember, to accomplish this magical act you must situate yourself outside your normal state of consciousness. You must identify with the Witness.

A good candidate for dissolution is pretense ... pretending to be something you're not or to know something you don't. Don't be discouraged when you finally face the truth of this pompous façade, because everyone you know is guilty too. Who doesn't stretch the truth a little, or spin a story to embellish the facts? It's a human condition, everyone does it, but the important thing is to be aware of yourself _doing_ it. With a little practice, and the corrective action of awareness, you'll understand the saying, "the truth will set you free."

I want you to understand something very important. All anxiety is based on the fear that someone will "find you out," see through the pretense of your false, egotistical self. All self-illusions must be protected, and the more you have to protect, the more anxiety you have to somehow cope with. Again, you must discard all useless baggage and just learn to be yourself. When you have nothing to protect, you have nothing to fear losing … then, only contentment remains. And one more thing. The *real you* is tens of times more attractive and powerful than any illusion the false self can dream up. Be yourself, that's all.

Chapter Five: Non-doing, Allowing

In the last lesson you learned the ancient secret of self-observation via the Witness ... in this lesson you will learn of its companion principle, Allowing. This is probably your key to the entire philosophy. Without it your progress may stagnate or grow only in spurts, but using it, you will change the world that you know.

Remember, everything you see or experience outside yourself is just a mirror that reflects the state of "being" inside. If your mind and emotions are peaceful, your world will reflect that peace. If however there is internal struggle, your world will reflect that self-same struggle and confusion back to you. In a sense, you are what you perceive outside yourself, and since no rational being would consciously harm himself/ herself, you must avoid resistance or struggle with what you see (what you are). First, you must pick up the signal the world is sending you – by being aware. Then, you have to do something ... or rather [by allowing] <u>not</u> do something.

You see, your tendency in the past has been to react in some way to what you see. Now that you're coming awake, you see the futility in the never-ending negative spiral you create by being "reactionary." It seems that Martin Luther King was onto something quite powerful, after all.

Keep in mind, you want to approach this like a scientist. Watch things closely, but always with detached curiosity. This includes everything that's happening outside, as well as everything that's happening inside…in response to everything that happens outside. It's all connected; one affects the other. If, however, you lose the scientist's edge and you become identified with your observation (emotional or otherwise) you lose the advantage. Your involvement places you on the same level as the "happening" and you get lost in the storm of action and reaction.

This does not mean that your approach to life should be like Spock from Star Trek; his character denied all feelings, exercised only logic, and was detached from all human-like tendencies. "There should be balance in all things," as the Zen and Tao masters remind. There's a time for watching, and a time for spontaneity (enjoying), but with both however, just "be aware."

Allowing is not just tolerating the things that annoy you. It may be that in the beginning, to gain a foothold, but what you're striving for goes beyond mere tolerating. You want to achieve balance with the annoyance, and if you're only tolerating its presence, your feelings toward it are still negative. By being aware of the negative reaction, each time it occurs, you are gradually "processing" or diluting its effect. In time you will have <u>no</u> reaction to that particular event, circumstance, or person, and you will be free of it ... balanced.

This brings us to a discussion about Freedom, what it really is. In this country we live with the illusion of being free, of living in Freedom. After all, it is written in our Constitution and backed by our system of laws. But ask yourself, do you really have the unconditional freedom to be or do exactly what you want? Of course not. To live in a society, they tell us, you must waive certain freedoms and conform to the accepted "standards" so that all runs smoothly. First ask yourself, is all running smoothly? Second ask yourself, do you have any [real] power to make things different? Again, they tell us, by your vote you hold the power to change all things. Wake up! What real power is one vote out of 250 million? Practically nothing.

But, want to know a secret? There is a way to live in society and have unconditional freedom. It works like the alchemy of olden times if you give it a chance. It will actually elevate you above the storms, the anxieties, and the agonies of society.

It works like this: Change your "awareness level" above that of common society, and you also change your "life level." Your Awareness Level, after all, is the only thing you [really] have any control of. Nobody but <u>you</u> controls how you think and perceive, and how you react, but this little bit of power, seemingly contrary to logic, is all you need to accomplish astounding change!

Look around you. Take a good look into the faces of all those busy worker citizens. Do you see smiles and contentment? Are their eyes shiny with awareness? Are they really living in the Now? You must admit, they're far from a state of self-liberty. They are like automatons, scurrying around, hypnotized by their fears and beliefs. They live on a common world, all are on the same limited Awareness Level. Is this anything like the fairy tale of liberty and freedom they believe they have?

If you can see this, you're already one step in awareness above that level. Do you have the courage to go further and actually live from a different world than you see? This different world holds not only the promise of true freedom, but the actuality of a state called self-liberty. And the first step in attaining this self-liberty is to detach, with awareness, from all those annoyances in the external world. You do this by Allowing.

Each day, as you become more accepting of what Is -- without judgment, without criticism – you will elevate your Awareness Level and magically transform your world. It sounds simple, and it is, but there's no greater force for change than the duality of <u>awareness</u> and <u>allowing.</u>

THE SECRET OF TRUE HAPPINESS IS TO CULTIVATE INNER LIBERTY

Are you aware that your mind is like a haunted house? The spirits of old memories fly through your mind uninvited; there are a hundred voices pulling you this way, pushing you that way, telling you what you should do, and what you shouldn't; desires come and go, no sooner is one satisfied than another takes its place; emotions spring from nowhere, to move you somewhere; thoughts come out of the blue, few serve any worthwhile purpose. Is it any wonder you feel trapped like a prisoner, with no way out?

But there is a way out. And it starts from the very place that gives you so much agony.

Start thinking of real freedom as a state of "inner liberty." Being free, inside first. You have to take control of your own mind again. Would you allow unwelcome intruders to stay in your house and bother you day and night? Of course not, so get rid of them! Your mind is like your house, it's where you live. But how do you reclaim what is yours? First, be watchful. Be very aware of each intruder as it enters your domain. Don't fight with it, don't argue with it, just watch … and soon it will leave.

Second, watch how you respond within, to what happens without. Don't let the outside get inside too. Accept and acknowledge what Is, without mental or emotional resistance, and you glide through life with the ***Flow of life***. Can you feel the truth of this? Take a moment and stretch your imagination a bit. See if you can feel how your life might change if your mind was peaceful. Instead of losing your head and over-reacting to some stressful situation, what would it be like to just watch and learn? … then take calm and appropriate action. Not only does this save a load of physical/emotional wear and tear, it influences everything on the outside as well. With habit and consistency, this simple process will transform both you and your world. Don't take my word for it, try it and see!

At first you're bound to stumble and fall, and feel awkward. But each time you fail, you are at least aware of the failure, and that in itself is a step toward the desired change. Try to mentally relate your anger and over-reaction to a wild tiger that breaks loose every so often. Most of the time you are caught completely off guard when it springs from its cage, doing damage before you can gather your wits. But from now on you will watch with awareness. You will feel it stir with resentment before it springs ... and each time you catch this tiger lunging out, you will have caught him in the act. And that, my friend, is how you tame the wild tiger!

There will be times, as you're treading this new path to self-liberty, that you won't know what to do – you won't have a clue of how to act or what to do – you will be confused and feel totally awkward. So what do you do? Nothing.

WHEN YOU DON'T KNOW HOW, STEP INTO THE NOW

It's really OK to do nothing at all. Just step into the moment. Feel your confusion, feel your awkwardness, feel your not-knowing. Don't try to *think* your way out as usual, but instead bear the discomfort of not knowing. Stand strong in that void, with only the Truth as your ally. And out of the void will come an answer. It won't come from thinking ...but from intuition ... or, the Universe may surprise you with an action of its own. Again, don't take my word for it. Try it!

We can call this the art of "not-doing." It seems totally contrary to all we've been taught, but a seed (from Truth itself) is contained in this art. It needs nurturing, it needs time to grow. But you won't believe the magical fruit that blossoms, then manifests into your reality. Let's look at some other examples of "not-doing."

Suppose that someone questions a fact or opinion you've recently expressed. Or worse, they call you a liar. You know what you would normally do – react! You would get angry, mount a defense of supporting evidence, rationalize, stretch the truth, and pull some poor unsuspecting bystander into the argument to support your view. Can you see the tiger lunging from its cage? Do you know the real identity of this tiger? It is called [Ego] the False self.

You know for yourself from past experience that:
1. this reaction caused you pain and stress;
2. it made you look foolish;
3. it did not prove or settle anything; and
4. it probably made for you an enemy who will taunt you further. So what was the point of all this? Who really benefited? The False self.

Now for contrast, let's see how a spiritually evolving person might handle this. First, be aware of the tiger stirring, the resentment and anger building. Second, do-nothing, delay the urge to react with a face-saving defense. Third, enter the moment, say nothing, stand there in the void and feel the truth of all that's passing through you. Fourth, if you do react, watch the effect it has on you and on others. Fifth, grow from the experience ... and let it go!

Isn't this a more mature and less stressful way of handling negativity? It works for negativity of all kinds. And the bonus is: your world changes as you change your mind.

The art of not-doing can also be extended to the way

you live life. Consider how often you think through and pre-plan each segment of your day, right down to the tiniest detail. Rarely do you do anything before it is first considered, thought through, planned, and re-considered. Living this way – only by thought – you miss the wonder of a level of life that happens all by itself, unfolding naturally with ease and spontaneity. To experience this natural *flow of life* however, you must first trust that such a level actually exists ... that animals, enlightened beings, even ET's and angels, all function on this level without care or concern of what will happen next. They have complete trust that all of life is unfolding for the greatest good of all, and that no egocentric thought is required to sustain them. Imagine the freedom of living this way.

This doesn't mean that thought is bad and has no place in this higher level life. Thought is a wonderful servant, but we have allowed it to become our master. When learning something new, thought is essential; when working with math to keep our lives and the budget balanced, thought is necessary; when using a recipe to cook a new dish, or just following a blueprint to build a new house, thought can serve us well. Used wisely it is a wonderful help, but when it constantly bothers us like a child with "what do we do next?" it becomes a tool of the False self, and its unending need for attention and stimulation.

***

WHEN YOU'RE IN THE NOW, DO-NOTHING BUT ALLOW

Try this experiment. Take just one day a week to try this. After several times you will likely find this practice most appealing, making you want to change your whole lifestyle to accommodate it. It goes like this:

First, firmly decide and affirm that you will allow this day to *flow* of its own accord, without any forethought or planning from you. You will take what you get … without judgment or criticism.

Second, you will step back from yourself and watch closely everything that happens. Be especially watchful of how the False self-reacts to negativity, and how the body feels afterward. Also notice how the False self characteristically "chases its tail" with meaningless chatter and thought.

Third, notice a pattern or an intelligence behind all that happens. It's almost as if you placed your life on auto-pilot and you're amazed to find that it *flies by itself*, without your constant supervision and input. In fact all flows quite smoothly, probably better and with less effort than would have been, had you been meddling as usual.

Fourth, decide to ally yourself with only the truth on this day. In other words, you will stand strong in that void, honestly feeling all that passes through you. You will not try to defend yourself by word or thought. If you are confused, you will *feel* confused … if you are angry, you will *feel* your anger … if you are afraid, you will *feel* your fear … if you are embarrassed about what others might think for just standing in silence, *feel* the embarrassment.

Fifth, "stand in the Now and just Allow." If you feel the spontaneous urge to do something or go somewhere, follow through. By trusting your feelings you are being receptive (accepting and allowing). However, a warning: Trust nothing that feels like guilt or anxiety or mere restlessness. These spring only from the False self.

This is really a wonderful, free way to live your life. Test it and see for yourself.

Chapter Six: Higher Thought

OK, so what is the difference between ordinary thought and higher thought? Remember, ordinary thought originates with the False self. That is its source. This kind of thought is based on the memory of all stored experience, book learning, and the opinions of others that you've accepted as your own. It's exactly like a computer: information in ☐ information out. If the material put in is faulty, the material that comes out (your reactions) is faulty. You've heard the expression "trash in equals trash out." I submit to you that most of what's been stored in that fabulous computer-brain of yours, has been faulty from the start. It's not the computer's fault, it is the fault of the operator, the False self. From [its] rather small viewpoint, it has selected material from its own small focus and called it fact; most of it was opinion though. So from your stand-point (the real you), can you see that you've been working with faulty material ... and you're practically programmed to fail?

Think of *common thought* as mechanical thought, because like a computer it only knows what it has stored in memory. In contrast, we have *higher thought* which is based on the all-encompassing viewpoint of Awareness. Common thought is egocentric and limited to the (stored) past, while higher thought considers the whole and is constantly updating itself with new information; it functions in the now as opposed to the past. The input of Awareness provides fact, not opinion, and it stimulates thought that is pure, not tainted.

Common thought, by its very nature, divides and separates. It classifies all things into polarities or opposites. This kind of thinking separates us from everything outside ourselves. From its polarized viewpoint, it constantly compares everything and everybody. All things are judged as good or bad, right or wrong; all things are quantified as large or small, rich or poor; all people are classified as friend or enemy. Do you see that this kind of thinking always forces you to take sides? To be <u>for</u> something, you must be against something else. To <u>be</u> someone, you must compare yourself to someone else. To be right, there has to be someone who's wrong. What happens when you take sides? You are forced to struggle against, to resist the opposite side. You already know this is useless. [You already know you're just fighting yourself.] This spawns never ending argument and resistance, never a solution. The best that can be hoped for is to compromise (to tolerate), and this never really satisfies anyone or solves anything … instead, it leaves festering resentment boiling beneath the surface.

So is there a way out? Is there another way to think?

You bet there is! It's above the polarities, it rests on balance, and it is never wrong. This third way of thinking is called Higher Thought ... Aware Thought ... Now Thought. All of these describe it to some measure, but with practice and application it becomes a kind of non-thinking, a Knowing. If you trust what you know, then there's no reason to think. And that is the state of awareness we're seeking.

Let's use an example. Suppose you go on a camping trip into the deep woods. You have taken three days' worth of food and supplies. After hiking a whole day you set up camp, store your food, and pitch a tent. The stars are bright, and you're blissfully tired, you fall into a deep sleep. In the morning you wake to find your camp has been rummaged and all your food has been stolen. Footprints nearby reveal the culprit, a bear. Do you panic, or do you enjoy the unexpected predicament? After all, that's what you came to the deep woods for anyway: an adventure to learn more about yourself, and a test of sorts, to prove the validity of these "truth teachings." You are hungry and you have no food. What to do? You noticed during the trek in, that the woods were full of wild nuts and berries. Some were poisonous, some were not. You wander through various patches of berries, picking and eating, enjoying the sweet fruits, with no care whether or not you've chosen the right ones. Why? Because you have experience in these woods and already <u>know</u> the edible berries. So, is there a choice to make? No. No person would consciously harm himself. Because you <u>know</u> which ones to eat, there is no thought, there is no choice.

The difference between truth and non-truth is a lot

like those wild berries. After a little exposure to the truth, it is easily recognized and its taste is eagerly sought. At this elevated stage of recognition there is no choice to make, therefore no thought required. Pick the berries, eat the fruit, enjoy the taste … and you're contented.

Higher thought is about wholeness. It does not divide and separate like its lower sibling. You see, right now you consist of divisions. Everything outside you is classified and quantified, named and labeled, judged right or wrong. Everything inside you is also partitioned similarly. You have a body, as opposed to spirit … you have a mind, as opposed to emotion … you have the conscious mind, opposed to subconscious mind … you have loving emotions versus hateful, angry emotions. In your life you have success and failure, friends and enemies, health and sickness, rightness and wrongness. With all these opposites struggling for recognition and dominance, is it any wonder that you're confused and disoriented?

But the good news is, there's a whole other way to live. It's as close as your breath, and as easy to take control of. It's as simple as changing your mind! It requires *intent*, first. Then practice, second. Your whole purpose is to change the way you think. And remember, you have an ally, a magic genie standing next to you, willing to serve. It's the Invisible Witness, the ***aware-will***. It is already whole, it is already free, it lives in the realm of higher thought and is always now present. This is the real you. Detach from the False self and assume your natural identity.

This talk about wholeness, and being one with

everything, scares a lot of people. They assume that if they shed the Ego they also shed their identity. Well, you do shed the lower identity -- the one that's false. But you re-gain the natural part of you that was lost. On the level of the True self [your spirit or soul] you retain your individuality. All your learning and growing, all your experience and talents from past lives remain your own, these provide the imprint of your very own unique character. This is your *individuality*, it is based on real experience, and your experience is shared with the Whole. But mere *identity* is a collection of labels, habits, beliefs, and attitudes; all are mere self-pictures, and all are false. They are false because they are only self-serving pictures and they disregard the Whole. When you become whole again, you are at peace, you are content…

Imagine what real wholeness is like. The little problems of day to day life fade into smaller perspective, they have no power to move you or to touch you. In real time, in the Now, you are already complete, perfect. The goals and strivings have resolved themselves (either in your favor or against), you have learned from their lessons and are at peace with the outcomes. The battles are over, the outcomes determined, and nothing from the past can touch you. The present is where you live but it is not static, unmoving … in fact every moment changes of itself, it blossoms into the new and unexpected.

See yourself in a world of fulfilled perfection. Imagine that all your desires and goals have been met. You are the exact ideal of everything you ever wished yourself to be. And yet, because all things must continue to grow and change, there is the tiniest impulse for something new ... new needs, new desires arise. But because you live in perfection, and the flow of life continues, all needs and desires are instantly satisfied. You never have to *reach* for anything!

You and Life are One. Unlike the old way, where there is you and a life (outside you) that must be shaped, managed, controlled ... now you are one with the flow of life and there is no separation. You are life, life is you, there is no need to struggle or control. There is no fear because there's nothing to fear. You do not fear, because you have no fear of yourself. Isn't wholeness great!

This world exists, and it's as close as a change in attitude.

Chapter Seven: The Golden Path

As we mentioned in the introduction there are a lot of paths to the aware, enlightened state we seek, but basically we can classify them in two categories. One can be referred to as the "masculine" or active way; the other can be called the "feminine" or passive way. These are two sides of the same coin, each relies on the other to exist ... though neither would admit such.

The left-hand path, or masculine way, takes an active hands-on approach to living life and developing awareness. All the "create your own reality" philosophies, and "learn by doing" concepts [even Science] fall into this category. Alchemy, magic, witchcraft, some forms of meditation and yoga, are all esoteric examples of the masculine approach. The will and imagination are all-powerful; the empowered self is a basic requirement.

The right-hand path, or feminine way, is passive and receptive. Fate and Destiny are accepted as the basic truth, everything has been pre-arranged, and an all-knowing God supervises the whole of creation without question or criticism. Christianity and the teachings of Mohammed are prime examples of this subjugative approach. God alone is all-powerful; trust and faith are strict requirements.

The Golden path is an integration of the right and left-hand paths, it holds the balance between these two polarities. This is the road less traveled, the golden mean, the Way that incurs no karmic debt. This is also the realm of the Witness, and the Third Way of thought. Life itself is all-powerful, the truest teacher ... and Truth is the only requirement.

Those who tread the Golden path use their very own lives as both the classroom and the teacher. No experience, whether positive or negative, is wasted. This path alone is above the plane of polarities, therefore all happenings, conditions, and experiences benefit the seeker. Imagine living life in the moment, welcoming whatever comes as a gift of spirit, knowing there is nothing to fear because you are one with life. This makes an unshakable foundation for the development of inner liberty and the experience of wholeness.

Can you see the continuity between the Golden Path and everything we've been speaking about so far? In fact, that is the test of the truth. If it is indeed truth, it will blend with or mix and match with any other aspect of truth. There are no discordant facts, no contrary explanations, no inconsistencies. You could lift out any paragraph -- or any chapter – and set it alongside any other paragraph or chapter, and you would find a seamless match. If it is all part of the same whole, the same truth, there can be no discontinuity. Again, try it.

What is a path? It's a way of life ... a way to view life, and a way to experience life. Unfortunately, in our culture, we haven't been presented many path choices to follow. The only ones we have been given (have inherited) are those that lead left or right. Science is a left brain, left hand path; Christianity is a right-brain, right hand path. Have we ever been encouraged to walk the middle way, straight ahead? Hardly.

Some people wonder, why tread a spiritual path at all? Is there any practical benefit for my day-to-day life? Of course there is. As emphasized before, the inner (spiritual) life relates to and drives the outer (circumstantial) life. If there is peace and harmony inside, there will be peace and harmony outside. I don't recommend it as a way of getting rich, which is an ego trap anyway ... the more money you have the more responsibility and headaches. But if a comfortable, secure, and peaceful life appeals to you this is definitely the way to go. You walk through life with ease and contentment, everything seems to magically fall into place without planning or forethought, circumstances and opportunities seem to come to you -- things you never dreamed of before as being satisfying. And best of all you are learning and growing at a rapid pace, with lessons specifically tailored to your individuality. Isn't this a much more sane and practical approach to life than what you're used to?

There are several common fallacies we grow up with, that are never challenged and rarely thought through. We need to look at these through the light of awareness, before treading the Golden path.

The first is success. We grow up with the idea that the purpose of life is to become a success. To be a success we must be rich, or famous, or stand out in some significant way. *We must be someone!* To be someone we must fight and struggle, plot and plan, compete to the very end. It's like we're all in a game that we have to play, whether we want to play or not. The rules are fuzzy. Some people have a moral code, a list of rights and wrongs that they try to abide by, but more often than not these people don't win the big prizes. The big winners, it seems, have no rules. They compete with cut-throat efficiency and anything goes. Their practiced smiles project an image of satisfaction and achievement … look at me, they silently mock. But if you could look deep into the core of his being, you'd see something very different. This person – and you can bet the house on it – is festering inside with fear and agony. He is driven, antagonized, and abused by something inside that will never give him a moment's peace … if he had sold his soul to the devil it would feel the same. What is this devil that drives him? It's a false image, i.e. the false self, the Ego.

It is painful to live from illusory pictures of who we are, instead of from reality. A man who pictures himself as a money-making genius will be upset by anything that contradicts that self-pleasing picture. If business becomes slow, as it will at times, it disrupts his pretentious self-image and causes internal distress. He worries what his friends will think, he worries if he can maintain the high style of living for his family. You see, the wider the gap between self-illusion and reality, the greater the pain. Reality is trying to teach him something about himself, hence the pain. But, in his mind, the "game" of making money gives him excitement and temporary pleasure -- false sensations, both. He is hooked on a drug sensation (emotional and hormonal) that becomes harder and harder to satisfy.

In the Game of Life there are winners and losers. If we call the person above a winner, is the loser any better off? Of course not. The loser is tortured by his own devils ... self-contempt, agony, and fear. And he is just as hooked on false sensations as the winner is. How much mileage in sympathy does he get from the "poor me" syndrome? This person wouldn't admit it but he gets a perverse pleasure from suffering the image of a loser.

If neither the winner nor the loser really win, is there any way out of the game? Is there another way to be a success? Yes. The middle way is the answer. The Golden path.

Imagine the "game of life" as a Football game. There are two teams, two opposing sides, each with its own plan (playbook) for winning the game. The players are very skillful at their individual tasks, and to them Football is the only way to live. Baseball or Basketball are whole other worlds ... different games for different people.

So they're all out on the field, butting heads, feeling the pain, but ignoring the pain for the sake of the Game. The tide flows first to one side, then to the other, back and forth, on and on, and no one knows for sure which side will win.

The "players" are all on the field. They represent the doers, the ground floor basic level of awareness.

Surrounding the game field is a stadium full of fans. They are emotionally aligned with one side or the other. They are not the doers, but are strongly identified with a side of their own. As the tide flows in favor of one side or the other, they feel the excitement then the agony. The fans aren't getting bloodied and dirty down on the field, in a sense they're a little smarter and so they represent a little higher level of awareness.

Back another step are the TV viewers at home watching the game. They are not in the stadium, they are feeling no pain, and they are not feeling the immediacy of emotions of the fans in their seats. The TV viewers are also identified with one side or the other but with less intensity and a little less agony. They're at a somewhat higher level of awareness ... but they are still in the Game.

If this makes any sense to you, can you see the place where you are in the Game?

Is there any way to *win* this crazy game? Yes, and the solution is simple. Don't play! Those who tread the Golden path have discovered, through their own awareness, that the only way to really win is to detach from useless human follies – like pride, vanity, and false ideas of success.

Let's go back to the football analogy for a moment. Where does the spiritually aware person fit into all this? He or she just enjoys watching the game ... they enjoy watching the people react to the game ... they enjoy watching the players play the game. They can come or go to the stadium, watch it on TV or a VCR, leave before the end, and really have no concern about who wins or loses. By not being involved with the results, he/she/they are free! Do you see the simple, bare truth in this?

The definition of real success is finally revealed. It's a simple matter to change your mind about success ... then start doing the things that make for real lasting success – and this is something you can take with you! You can't take your *stuff* with you when the Game is done.

SUCCESS IS A MATTER OF DETACHMENT, NOT ACCUMULATION...

Another common fallacy is the idea that we must always impress others. Somehow it has become deeply ingrained that if we don't make a meaningful impression on others, we lose points in the big game. A lot of this ties into the previous fallacy that we must be successful. But aside from that, there are even deeper reasons for wanting to impress ... and all of these spring from fear.

We fear being alone, and we'll do anything it takes to maintain a friendship, a relationship, a partnership, or whatever. And if we lose all that, all the positive forms of companionship, we will revert to the negative just to attract some form of attention from others. Getting in trouble, showing off, being obnoxious are all forms of negative attention. Do you see how the fear of being alone drives us to do anything we have to, to stay out of its void? {The cure for being lonesome, remember, is to be aware of the void it creates, feel the feeling, and let it pass.}

You may want things from other people: sex, money, compliments, approval, the pride of being seen with him or her. The list goes on, but what always remains is the craving need to have others validate our existence. This is insane ... because you exist and have value regardless of what other people think. Let me tell you a truth you've probably never considered: You are chained to anyone you want something from. In other words, they control you. Conversely you can do, be, or say anything you want around someone you want nothing from. You are free. Think about it!

Watch how you feel when in the presence of someone you want something from. Then watch how you feel when in the presence of someone you want nothing from. In which case are you more at ease and natural – just being yourself?

So what is the remedy for trying to impress others? First remember, you are independent of all others ... the Universe will support you (if you allow it) regardless of what you think you need from others. Next, notice how easily you let other people tell you how to feel. A sarcastic remark, a sour face, or a rolling of eyes will make you wonder what they're thinking of you, and always make you feel bad. Why suffer their foolishness? Let it go... And finally, watch how unnatural you feel and act (putting on the fake face) when others approach. Ask yourself, "Why do I change?" "What do I want from this person that makes me act unnatural?" If you want a good example of how a spiritual person handles peer pressure and the influence of others, remember this: *"What does the Eagle care, what the ground creatures think of him?"* When you are real, there's no need to be impressive ... it comes with the territory.

CHAPTER EIGHT: SELF-TRANSFORMATION
(Dissolving the False Self)

This brings us to the most important part of our work. Self-transformation is the process of detaching from the Ego or false self. To accomplish this feat and claim the prize you cannot "resist" the ego, you cannot "deny" the ego, and you cannot merely "wish" that it go away. The only thing you can do is process (integrate) it back into the wholeness of your Being. By simply eliminating its source of power, you essentially dissolve it back into essence.

Right up to this very point in your life you have identified with the False self. It has been the only You that you have known. Now you can see another option. You have a transitional self that is a master Alchemist, an ally, and a friend. It alone has the power to dissolve the Ego and deliver you back to your True being.

The Invisible Witness is your ticket home. Like the Ego, it is not your real Self. It is a projection of your real essence though, a useful tool or vehicle, and since its nature is balanced awareness, it is closer by far to the real You. If you will step into this aspect of yourself, you will be closer to home than ever before. That's what transformation is all about.

The power of the Witness to transform, is in the present. You've heard this expression before: "The power is in the present." But do you really grasp the meaning of this?

You can understand now that memory of the past and imagination of the future are pure illusions. The only place they're happening is in your head! But Now is the only place that is anchored to reality; what happens in the Now is what is happening in reality. What happens in reality is Truth (fact). When you are "lost in thought" of the past, or the future, you are in fact still in the Now – but lost in an illusion. Is that clear?

People say the Past has a power over them … others say the Future holds the power. Don't you see that both these concepts are wrong? The Past is a collection of stored memories that draw their power through You (in the present). The Future is an imagined projection, based on stored memories, that draw their power through You (in the present). So where is the power? Where it always was: in the Present! The real You resides in the Now.

If you would only live your life in the present, as a child lives and plays in the present, you would re-discover the wonder and amazement of real life -- and the abundant power available to all who play there. And there is more than enough power for everyone. Would you think the sun shines more for some people than others? It shines in abundance for everyone who's outside.

In this lesson we want to focus on Transformation, and I want to give you the most powerful techniques to help you accomplish the ultimate transformation: dissolution of the false self.

- ❖ The first two techniques have to do with Time Awareness, or moment awareness. You now realize the importance of the Present moment, you realize it is the source of all power, and you realize that the longer you can stay "aligned" with the moment, the more you will transform yourself and your world. Therefore your first assignment is to be conscious of as many moments of your day as you possibly can. You may only succeed a few times at first, then more and more, as you become more skillful. Each moment of conscious awareness will be like a single pearl. Your job is to string together as many pearls as you can, then you will have an unbroken string – and a new awareness!!

To do this, first remind yourself to step into the Witness. Observe where you are and what you are doing. Do not criticize or judge your actions, merely observe. As a special signal to remind yourself , use this: BECOME CONSCIOUS whenever you feel UPSET, ANGRY, or NERVOUS. Then ask yourself, "Where am I, and what am I doing (or thinking)?"

That's all you have to do at first. But realize, you are observing the False self. Only the False self feels hurt! Remember your purpose: you are 'taming the tiger' of the mind and dissolving the Ego self. We might call the above technique, "stringing the black pearl necklace."

And guys, if this is uncomfortable for you, think of it as a "shaman's string of power beads."

Next technique: "stringing the white pearl necklace." After a little practice with the previous technique, maybe after a week or so, add this one too. We are still practicing moment awareness. But with this aspect of the technique, we want to become aware of the moments that we deliberately choose. This is a kind of "waking meditation."

During parts of your day become deliberately conscious of the moment. Step into the Witness awareness and just observe. Where are you? What are you doing? Catch yourself in a spontaneous setting, just doing what you do. Again, do not judge your actions as good or bad. Observe. The most mundane moments are probably the best ... like making the bed, tending the garden, talking on the phone, driving the car. Choose the routine parts of your day that usually go by unnoticed. After you become proficient at waking up to the routine parts of your day, also include moments that are playful and joyous, active or serene. All these are "white pearl" moments you want to string together.

By carefully attending to the above dual-techniques you are gathering power and stabilizing your awareness within the Witness. Very powerful stuff here!

❖ The next transformation exercise deals with stopping thought. Have you ever had a problem or concern that your mind just won't let go of? It seems no matter how hard you try to think of something else, this "invader" keeps coming back to drain your energy and steal your mental focus. It chases round and round in your mind (like a dog chasing its tail) then comes back again from a whole new direction or perspective. What a pest! What can you do to break the annoyance? And what does this have to do with transformation?

Answering the last question first, transformation is a process of mind clearing. As long as the false self has free reign to run your mental domain, you are still in a fog, still in a state of forced hypnosis. The "invader" is of course caused by our old nemesis, the false self. This is one of its tricks designed to steal your energy and keep you occupied in a useless pursuit. You must wrestle back the power and take charge of your own mind.

Now, what can you do to break this influence? Simply stop feeding it thought energy with your precious attention. Stop thinking! Take a five minute time out, find a quiet place, and make your mind an empty chalice. "Only an empty chalice can be filled." You will empty the contents of the old and refill it with the refreshing energies of clarity and purity. Unless you've spent long hours in practice of meditation, this may be somewhat difficult at first. When you first quiet the mind, other thoughts, other problems, other concerns may also try to intrude. Just be aware of them trying to distract you and refuse them admittance with absolute authority. Here is the secret:

STOP ALL THOUGHT.

MAINTAIN YOUR INTENTION TO DO SO.

TURN YOUR FOCUS TO FEELING INSTEAD.

Become aware of the feeling of your body. Or the

feeling of the subtle energy that courses through your body. Or just feel yourself breathing. Feel, don't think! Become an empty vessel...

Within five minutes your mind will be settled, and it will be yours again!

❖ Continuing to the next transformation technique, we go back to the non-resistance concept. I dislike the use of this phrase because of its obvious origin, but "resist not evil" may help you gain a better grasp of this. In our work of transformation it is absolutely necessary that we adopt this attitude of non-struggle with the outside world. You have to realize that your struggle with the exterior is a symbol and reflection of your struggle with annoying elements within. Also remember that the outer symbol you struggle with is a key to what you're resisting or fighting within you.

Example: Suppose you struggle daily with other people. You find yourself criticizing their stupidity, their ego, and self-serving actions. You do this in silence, talking to yourself. (By the way who is suffering, who is hurting the most? You or them.) This is a very natural struggle to those on the spiritual path, starting to wake up. As you become more aware of the Truth, it becomes difficult to tolerate the pettiness and lack of rational thought in others. It's OK if you see these things in others without criticism, as merely objective facts. But for the most part you are "projecting" your own internal struggle onto those around you. This is OK too if you realize you are "projecting" instead of observing. It's all for learning. But what are you trying to tell yourself about yourself? Your struggle is with your own Ego. This is not the way to make it go away, because you empower what you resist.

What other things do you commonly struggle with? Fortune, fame, popularity? Time, business, success? Love, affection, romance? Old age, good looks, obsession with health? Take a close look at these common everyday concerns. I ask you, what do they all have in common? EGO.

The solution to all these problems, concerns, and struggles comes from a higher level. Do not resist. Step into the moment. Stop all thought. Trust. When you do this something magical happens because you entrust the ultimate solution to a level higher, one above ordinary thought. Whereas before, you only trusted what you yourself thought through, from your own conditioned mind. The higher solutions will come to you but you must be patient, and you must trust. This is a secret you can take to the bank!

Again, you may ask: "What has this to do with transformation?" Stop struggling with your False Self and you will see—

- ❖ Here's a technique I found by accident – although there really are none – while practicing a form of "feel good" meditation. For that reason, we'll call it the "feel good" technique. It will deliver you to a place of high intensity energy that by its very nature is transformative.

First – here's a mental concept for you to understand. Be very clear on this: Conscious thinking is as different from Awareness as salt is from sugar. They are two totally different states. Since you identify yourself mostly with your thinking, you conclude that your thought and awareness are the same thing. They are not. Thought belongs to the lower self on the level of the material plane. Awareness however belongs to the higher self on levels above the material plane.

To be Aware in the true sense, all thought must stop. You "feel" yourself in the moment as you "sense" signals coming from both the external environment, and the inside as well. In other words you have a strong sense of your individual Being in the here and now, and at the same time you are attuned and sensitive to all that's happening within and without. The pure state is hard to describe in words, but it's a little like waking up in the night after a noise in the house disturbs your sleep, and listening so intently with all your senses focused for the slightest noise or out of place sound. Pure Awareness is that focused, but without the alarm and tension of the above example.

As with the thought stopping technique, set aside at least five minutes or more where you can be by yourself, undisturbed. Make your mind an empty chalice by stopping all thought. Just feel your Being in the moment with no thought whatever. Gradually you will notice a strong sense of yourself just Being. Be aware of everything, both inside and out. Now realize that in the truest, purist part of YOU there is a "sweet spot" as golfers and baseball batters refer to that rare place where the ball, the club, and the person become one. In every person there is a place that feels right, it feels balanced, it feels good. Without thinking, use your feeling sense to search out this one pure spot. When you attune to it there will be no doubt. It will feel like rapture, allurement, bliss, or sensuality. Keep the power of your full awareness there, and let it expand. Do remember to come back to this world!

❖ Another Transformation exercise comes to us from the Don Juan Teachings of Carlos Castaneda. I've found it very effective at putting things in proper perspective, while keeping the immediacy of the moment a priority. It is called "making death an ally." It works like this: Imagine you have just found that you have less than a week to live. How will you live your last few days?

Most would be shocked and would withdraw into a shell to wait for the end to come, much the same as they do day to day already. These unfortunate ones are so shell-shocked with life anyway -- they toil through each day in a hypnotic slumber -- that little would change for them regardless. A few of these however, may finally get the point and emerge into the light.

Most of us though, the spiritual souls, would enter a state of near enlightenment. Knowing the end was really at hand, we would do a mental up-shift, quickly alter our lives, and change our perspectives. We suddenly know what our priorities are: what is most important and in what order. We become "clear" about ourselves and unburdened by useless cares and issues.

This is a useful exercise to practice when we find ourselves confused and overly burdened by the "artificial" demands of life. It shocks the petty (false) self out of the way so the light of reason can prevail. This is just another tool to pry us lose from the tyranny of an artificial viewpoint.

The lesson here is to live each day like it might be your last, because one day it will be.

- ❖ Now we come to one of the most practical and easy to accomplish techniques that I have found. It is easy to remember and easy to use in your everyday life, but at the same time it is a powerhouse of energy for change and transformation.

How many times a day do you find yourself literally butting heads with reality? For all but the spiritually-minded that's exactly what the majority do. And that's exactly why they are so exhausted by day's end. Here are two little words that I want you to remember:

ACKNOWLEDGE AND ACCEPT!

These can work magic if you'll remember to apply them each time you feel stressed or are resisting something. Let me explain. When you encounter a resistance of any kind, first "acknowledge" that it is. (It is what it is, avoid labeling it as bad.) This sounds simple but you'd be surprised how many uncomfortable things you just ignore and suppress. The false self is very cunning at hiding our hurts, letting them build inside, until one day the festering manifests into a major problem. Don't let this happen! Always see and acknowledge what hurts you and short-circuit the old suppression trick. Also by acknowledging a problem you ally yourself with Truth, with Reality. Remember to stand firm, feel the feelings, watch your reactions ... you may be standing in a void, but remember, Truth is the strongest ally.

The second part of the formula is to "accept." Does this word sound familiar? It should, because this is a close relative of "allowing." By accepting "what is" you allow it to be, without condition or judgment. And this is where the magic of real transformation begins. By refusing to wrestle, resist, oppose, or deny – you become indifferent to its power to torment you.

Whatever you're indifferent to has no power to affect you!

As an example, suppose you just found out that you've been passed by for a promotion that you were expecting. This would likely be a very stressful situation, something you would normally wrestle with, resist, and try to fix blame. Don't do that! Remember you're a spiritual person on the Golden Path and you refuse to act like everyone else would.

Acknowledge the fact: You didn't get the job you expected, and you feel a temporary flare of anger. OK, no problem. It is what it is … I refuse to label it as 'bad' … and I refuse to hide the hurt. Sure, my ego has been bruised – but hey, whatever hurts the ego is good for the real me! This was a lesson I needed to learn, that's why I attracted it. One for me, one less for ego.

You see? Just talk to yourself. Turn a lemon into lemonade. You win!

Now you can Accept what is. You allow it to be, without condition, without judgment, without excuse. Your indifference to its negative side has neutralized its power to further affect you. Advance three paces on the Golden Path. You have just "transformed" a host of old feelings that have haunted you for years. They were clustered together and called inferiority.

❖ And finally for this lesson, we will consider a subject

that is near and dear to everyone. It is called physical rejuvenation, finding the fountain of youth within. You have heard the phrase, "Youth is wasted on the young." So true. They have all the vibrancy, energy, and enthusiasm but lack the wisdom to make the most of life. They take the gift of youth for granted. This is another paradox of physical life that seems totally backwards. But the solution to any physical paradox is found on the spiritual level.

You'll remember that there is a natural order to things, a continuity. Things flow from inner to outer ... from thought and imagination first, to action last ... from consciousness first, to the physical level last. When you're working with transformation, the same order must be followed. You have heard before that "youth is a state of mind." Well, it does start there. We have all known people who in their seventies and eighties still seemed spry, alert, and full of energy. We wondered if they had a secret. But no, I doubt that even they knew what kept them young. You see, they were too busy enjoying life to even be concerned. And that in itself is a secret of staying youthful – being indifferent to old age (unconcerned).

Those who fight and curse and struggle with approaching old age only hasten the process. The vanity of the false self is another of its own self-destructive mechanisms. Be aware of this. OK, you say, this is fine knowing how to not hasten the aging process. But is there a way to reverse the aging my body has already endured and win back that lean, supple, and vigorous body I once had? Thirty years ago I would have said, no.

Today we live in a time of great change. There is an acceleration of energies on the planet that have not occurred here since the last time human consciousness leaped to another level. Thirty to forty thousand years ago our ancestors, the Neanderthals, barely stood upright. They were ugly and hairy, big boned, barely conscious and severely retarded. But something happened, it still has our scientists stumped, something that brought about a glorious transformation of this ugly creature. Suddenly a new creature emerged from the old. It stood fully upright, was beautifully proportioned and hairless. But most amazing, it had a remarkable intelligence unlike anything to emerge from an earth species. This new man was called Cro-Magnon, and our scientists are still debating how this miracle in evolution could have possibly occurred in so short a time span. I believe a quickening of human consciousness is again rapidly approaching physical manifestation. We are about to evolve again into an even more amazing species – with a higher consciousness and body to match.

So you see why I believe that total rejuvenation of the mind and the body are now real possibilities. But not for everyone. There are those among us whose thinking and spiritual development is still retarded. Because they have done nothing to advance their essence, their consciousness, they will not be a part of this glorious species transformation. This is not an elitist belief but a statement of fact. Look around you, there will be precious few who will actually make this transition. Archeology has discovered that, back then, the two species had coexisted together for quite some time before the lesser species (Neanderthal) began to disappear. The same will occur in this time of consciousness transformation.

This information is a slight digression, so we'll leave this subject for now and return to it in another lesson. What I want to stress is that we live in a test tube environment of unimagined possibilities, and transforming energies that we can use at will. Reverse aging is possible, but it first requires the belief of such. As always, it must follow the natural order from inner to outer. If rejuvenation of your present physical body is a priority, then by all means "do what feels good."

CHAPTER NINE: "ATTACHED TEMPORARY ENTITIES"
(FURTHER UNRAVELING THE FALSE SELF)

To re-state the opening of our last lesson: Self transformation is the process of detaching from the Ego or False Self. To accomplish this feat and claim the prize you cannot "resist" the ego -- you cannot "deny" the ego -- and you cannot merely "wish" that it go away. The only thing you can do is process (integrate) it back into the wholeness of your Being. By simply eliminating its source of power, you essentially dissolve it back into essence.

I want to continue the work of the previous chapter by providing more information about the workings and structure of the false self, and provide a secret exclusive process. The more familiar we become with this devious and deceitful "attachment" to our minds, the better equipped we are to disable its structure and dissolve it back into nothingness.

For those of you who studied or might have read the early channeled works of Seth (The Seth Material, etc.)

you will find this familiar. One part of the philosophy of Seth dealt with, what he called, "Aspects" of personality. These were seen as individual facets of a person's whole personality; each had an identity exclusive of the other facets; and each had the ability to "take over" without being noticed. This is similar to the Multiple Personality syndrome we often hear about, but shockingly, common to all of us.

Each of these *aspects* had a dominate trait, like anger or timidity, aggressive or passive, outgoing or withdrawn, athletic or cerebral, (and even more basic traits like revenge, pride, deceit, or nurturing, compassionate, helpful, etc.) and so on... But the trait displayed at any one moment, defined the individual in that moment. Have you ever watched a friend change to someone completely different right before your eyes? Each aspect, as you can see, has its opposite -- and these opposites are constantly in conflict within the personality. The continual conflict inside makes the mind a battlefield of competing influences. And this is why people feel anxious or tense without really knowing why.

Seth hinted that these individual traits or temperaments were the dominant personality structure of one of that soul's previous incarnations ... that an *Oversoul* watched over these individual parts, supervising their ongoing growth, and was the repository for their separate histories and identities. This philosophy introduced some of our favorite concepts like: soul mates, group souls, and individual souls attached to a common Oversoul. In other words, you are not just one soul but part of a family of souls, like branches of a tree. Some souls were destined to venture forth and become independent Oversouls (like the Sovereign Entity, in *WingMakers* site).

But back to the individual personality structure-- These separate aspects are like satellites revolving around a main body, the Mind, waiting for an appropriate opportunity or condition to call it forth into action. Example: Suppose you're on the way to work in the morning, minding your own business, thinking about things to do at work. This is one *aspect*, by the way, doing the driving for you. It has been conditioned through many years of road experience to handle the driving responsibilities while another part of you plans the day. Now all of a sudden another driver races around you, gives you a finger sign, and cuts into your lane -- so close that you have to apply brakes and skid sideways. What happens to You?

You have an awful reaction and a sudden shift of personality. At the moment of reaction another aspect hops into the driver's seat. You are swept away by emotions of anger and revenge. If you could step back and watch yourself (which is exactly what you should do) you would witness a crazy wild-man or bitch laying on the horn, flipping naughty hand and arm gestures, and mouthing threatening words to the evil-doer ahead. Now, according to the degree of your anger, or the coming awake of your true self in that moment, the incident will either escalate or dissipate. This is an extreme example, of course, but one wherein you can readily identify with the dramatic shift. Other shifts however are more subtle and even less noticeable. But they do occur and it is your responsibility to catch them in the act. Each time you do, there's a bit of a scorching (by the light of awareness) to this un-mature aspect -- and a more general scorching to the False Self as a whole.

You can see that the false self, in its never ending tricks to deceive, is trying to imitate the reality of the spiritual plane. This is its own form of "disinformation" that's so often effectively employed by government intelligence agencies: i.e., mix a little truth with a lot of fiction and somehow the whole farce is more easily accepted as fact. By establishing itself in your mind as an oversoul with many faces (aspects), it pretends to be the supreme authority of your own psychological world. Moreover, you unknowingly "identify" with its false life and each of its artificial personalities. The transition from one false aspect to another is so smooth and convincing, that you believe you are same whole person (the Singularity) with each switch. But you are not. The real YOU is lost in a fog of thought and emotion supplied by each false aspect. The irony is, it is all your own energy, freely given to help deceive yourself. In essence, you're asleep at the wheel!

I'd like to give you a mental peg to help you remember what an aspect really is: ASPECT or ASPE(CT). Let's break the word down into its basic parts:

A: Attached
S: Separate
P: Personality
E: Entity
C: Conditioned
T: Temporary

Guy Finley's excellent book on this same subject, "The Intimate Enemy," calls these troublesome aspects TPIC's. This stands for Temporary Person In Charge. Their lives indeed are temporary and fading, lasting only as long as the condition or circumstance which called them forth persists ... then another TPIC replaces it, responding to its own call from the external world. While a specific Temporary is in charge, running its own show, it has very little memory of the others it has replaced, nor of their specific intentions or desires. Each is an ego unto itself.

Here is where the internal conflict begins. Each of these temporary aspects seems to have an agenda of its own. As an example suppose you discover – either through the comment of another or by personal observation – that you've put on a few extra pounds and obviously it detracts from your ideal image. This circumstance (awareness of your overweight condition) signals the "ideal image aspect" to respond. An unperceived switch occurs and a sudden overwhelming desire invades your psychological atmosphere. You must lose weight! You look through the diet books, selecting one that might work; you consider a new exercise regimen; you look through magazines, considering a new wardrobe for the new you while admiring all those slender models. You promise yourself, "This time I'm going to devote all my energies to looking good, eating right, and feeling good about myself again!"

The phone rings. A friend is calling. She tells you there's a new restaurant in the mall that everyone is raving about. "Come on," she insists, "what else do you have to do today? I hear it's a singles hangout too." This circumstance calls forth another aspect – Fun Nancy. She could care less about how great she looks – she's already convinced she is. The only things that occupy her mind are to eat, drink, flirt, and be happy. So off she goes to the mall. Nancy is in; Bertha is out. And so are Bertha's firm intentions. *Ladies, this is intended only as a simple example that everyone can relate to. There are a LOT of guys with this problem too.

Here is a story from Guy Finley, found in his book, "The Intimate Enemy." This concerns an incident he observed in a restaurant. "On this particular occasion, Guy noticed three men dining at a nearby table who were busy gossiping and bragging about themselves. One of the men, who did his best to monopolize the conversation, boasted about how well his life was going. When the waiter asked if he wanted to order a drink, he claimed self-righteously to his friends that he had overcome his drinking problem and did not drink anymore. After the meal was over, two of the men left, leaving behind the one who had been doing most of the talking. Within a few minutes a fourth man entered and joined the first, who now seemed to undergo a drastic change. This man, who only moments before had seemed so carefree, now proceeded to sadly relate some disturbing events from his past. And as he continued to talk over his difficulties, this same man who earlier that evening had proclaimed to the first group that he no longer drank, now ordered several drinks! It was as though he had no memory of who he had been only moments earlier. He had actually become a different person in the span of less than five minutes.

"Guy explained … None of us is a singular, whole

person. Rather, each of us is a plurality, made up of many selves, but convinced we are a singularity. At any moment a different self can take the stage, and while it reigns it believes fully that it is the actual, complete person. But in fact, none of these selves is real. Each is no more than the creation of a temporary conjunction of conditions... From one minute to the next our values and desires can change, depending on which TPIC is in charge...

"As each of these secret selves tries to prove its permanent and real, it necessarily comes into conflict with other contradictory ones. Yet, each TPIC remains ignorant of the existence of the others. As a result, the division within our Self becomes deeper and gives rise to more unconscious discomfort." End of Guy's quotes.

You can see what you're up against here; it seems the deck is fully loaded against you. Not only is there a False Self to keep in check and monitor, but there are many! I know you're thinking the task seems insurmountable, so why bother. The good news is – you now have the upper hand because you're *aware* of the False Self's most cunning and deceitful trick. All those costume changes (to different personalities) are just a distraction to keep your mind occupied with different desires, and their associated thoughts and emotions. By knowing this, and by being aware each time a change to a different façade occurs, you accelerate the process of dissolution of the entire false structure. So don't be further discouraged by the task ahead, be further encouraged.

There is one more point I'd like to make before closing this subject. You now have a reason to forgive all those people – family, friends, associates, enemies – who have wronged you in the past. It really wasn't them! It was instead an artificial entity, making a temporary appearance, to respond to something that you did. And that's all it was; just a response to a perceived threat, insult, or judgment, hastily made by one your own false aspects. Simple as that. Case closed. Let it go.

Chapter Ten: The "Perfect" Meditation

Have you ever had one of those magical days where everything seemed to go your way? Unexpected opportunities just fell into your lap, and people—even strangers—showered you with uncommon attention and compliments. You knew that something unusual and rare was happening, but you didn't know what.

The next day, probably, things returned to normal and that sense of magic was gone. What had happened? Was it some cruel cosmic joke ... or was it something that, maybe, you could call upon again?

I tend to believe that this charmed state is an aspect of a larger, encompassing state of consciousness that we all possess, but for reasons of fixation of the lower mind to earthly matters, we unknowingly block. Under the right conditions we can let go the fixation, free the higher mind, and gradually re-learn to maintain this new consciousness and charmed state of awareness.

This is called being "in the flow." It has also been

called "being centered." An age-old Mediterranean concept, referred to as the *baraka*, equates this to simply flowing with the river of life. One is either on or off the *baraka*. When you are on you can do no wrong and everything proceeds with a magical perfection. When you are off things are left to chance and few things go as intended. According to the concept, as you let go the intention to make things happen and instead allow the inflow of higher will, you will always be delighted with where you land. Riding the *baraka* is like an adventure, everything you encounter is a personal lesson, a timeless pearl of wisdom made for you alone.

Simply stated, to go with the flow you must detach from the ingrained mindset, to make things happen. Second, you have to trust God, the Universe, your higher Self, or whatever, as the source of your life—a beneficent all-knowing force, willing and determined to guide you to your highest good. If you can pull back several times a day, and remind yourself to LET GO and TRUST, you will be taking the first step in sailing the magical *baraka*.

The next step however is the most important. It involves making a connection, a channel, to this higher source of power and guiding wisdom. To do this you must learn to meditate correctly—or at least effectively.

There are people who are excellent meditators. They can center their mind upon a single idea and hold it without wavering for twenty minutes or more. This simple practice has numerous physical and psychological benefits, all documented and proven by scientific study. That's fine. But beyond being able to hold a prolonged thought, what else have they accomplished mentally or spiritually with that marvelous, disciplined mind? Not much. They must also expand the limits of this "thoughtless" state and explore the outer reaches of consciousness. Some meditators may well have done so, I can't say, but the point is, there is much more to meditation than fixation of thought.

Remember these two truths:
1. The most basic purpose of meditation is to raise the personal vibrations of self.
2. The ultimate purpose of meditation is to connect with the higher Self, God, or higher will.

If you meditate correctly you will accomplish first one, and then the other of these two objectives.

In raising the personal vibrations you render yourself almost invisible to the hard knocks of everyday life. Worrisome problems and common negativity seem to pass right through you. And if they do touch you, it is but lightly.

Compare a ball of clay to a feather. Both are subject to the same physical laws (gravity, inertia and such). Drop them both from a high place and watch how the earth (physical life) reacts to each one. The ball splatters, but the feather lands lightly. A person who meditates on a regular basis raises his or her vibrations and becomes like a feather.

Once you've accomplished raising your vibrations above a certain level, another advantage becomes instantly apparent. One day, suddenly, you will achieve a spectacular breakthrough to your higher mind. It can take many forms, but most people become aware of a blinding light in their head, a euphoric rush of energy, and a sense of noble presence surrounding their entire being. It is a momentous occasion that will never be forgotten, and from that time on you will live an almost charmed existence. You have been touched by the gods.

I once knew a fellow, a client of mine, who had read scores of books on self-hypnosis, and he'd tried the many experiments outlined in those books. He was really onto something, he assured me, but he needed help to go deeper. He wanted to establish a firm contact with a "most exhilarating presence" he'd discovered inside himself.

As a practicing hypnotherapist I'd encountered many strange requests, but this man's enthusiasm was so uncommon I just had to probe deeper. I asked him to tell me more.

According to him, he had read a new book about expanded states of hypnosis, and it suggested a self-hypnotic exercise that promised a profound state of consciousness. It required the subject to sit in an upright relaxed position, breathe deeply for several minutes, then to visualize the most "perfect" place in the world; it was to be an isolated place where you could be totally free and uninhibited. The key word to the whole procedure however was "perfect"… and he went with it.

He began to imagine his perfect place: an isolated island in a far off sea, a beautiful beach, lush palms and rich vegetation, a surrounding reef of crystal clear water. He saw and imagined himself in a perfect body, breathing the freshest, most scintillating air. As he concentrated, the world around him began transforming into a dream-world of ecstatic perfection.

Soon the feeling of perfection seemed to grow and

expand, taking on a life of its own.

And then it happened! He felt a shift occur inside, like a part of his mind had come alive. There was a rush of excitement, a feeling of overwhelming exhilaration—and a perfect presence stood before him. It was the most noble, loving presence he'd ever felt. An emotional sense predominated, it was more a feeling than an image. Lasting for mere seconds, it dissolved back into the ethers from whence it came.

But an obsession remained long after the experience. He had to reach it again! He tried several more times on his own, but failed to re-establish the contact. The blame, he thought, was his inability to fully relax again. So he came to me.

He wanted merely to be placed back into hypnosis, using the procedure he had used successfully, and be given a post-hypnotic cue that he could use for himself to re-establish the connection to his "presence."

I did this for him, successfully, and he went happily home. A week later he called to thank me. He said everything was fine, that the procedure had worked great, and that he'd connected firmly with that part of himself that was so loving and full of power. Although he seemed coy in relating more details, I knew his presence would be a source of help and guidance beyond anything I could offer further.

But he had unknowingly given me the seed for a technique that time and again I have used with great success to help others find the flow, the exhilaration of their own energy source. It works, and I'm going to share it with you.

Find a time and place where you can be alone and remain undisturbed for about twenty minutes. Just sit down on something comfortable. Keep your feet on the floor and sit up straight. Begin breathing in and out, nice and slow. Fill your lungs deeply. Do this for a minute, or until you begin to feel light-headed. It will be a pleasant and relaxing feeling.

Do you remember when, as a child, you could easily play games of "pretend?" Your imagination was so lively that you could make believe almost anything, and make it so. That's exactly the kind of imagination I want you to use now. Make this exercise a fun, child-like game.

Now clear yourself. Let go all the problems of the day, all the tugs on your mind and consciousness, all the things you haven't done or should do. See an old chest, like a pirate's strongbox, before you. Dump all the heavy mental stuff in there and close the lid. Turn away.

See before you a shimmering window, a force-field of pulsating energy. It is an energy portal in the fabric of time, a door into a perfect reality/ dimension. See it clearly with your mind's eye, feel its scintillating energy vibrating before you. Pretend it is so, and make it so!

Now step through, into the other side. As you pass through, a very peculiar thing happens ... you have magically transported yourself eons of time into the future, your consciousness has instantly transformed into the ideal, fully evolved you. You are at peace with yourself and your god, in fact, you have become the god of you, the I AM presence. You have absolute freedom to do, to be, to have anything you could possibly desire. Nothing can be denied you.

In this perfected, ideal reality (which really does exist by the way) you feel only emotions of pleasure, joy, and ecstasy. Pain, anger, and depression simply do not exist here; they only exist in the world you've left behind. Really feel and imagine - pretend - that you feel all this joy and pleasure bubbling up inside you, welling up from the crystal spring of your most pure, inner being.

At this point in the exercise the use of "intent" becomes so important. The old axiom that "energy follows thought" becomes even more pronounced when you're in this altered state. Wherever you focus your mind, with clear intent, the mind will go and attune you to the object of that intent. Intend to attune your mind to the emotions of joy and pleasure ... and soon you will actually feel them bubbling to the surface.

Next begin to dwell on the idea of "perfection." Intend to feel it all around you. You are now in a place where every happening, every circumstance, and everything you encounter is as perfect as God intended it to be. A leaf never falls in the wrong place, a grain of sand is never where it should not be. Everything is in perfect order!

Understand that it is only the misguided thoughts and beliefs of man, in the outer world, that have introduced the only disharmony and imperfection there is. In the higher worlds, disconnected from man's ego and misunderstanding, there exist only the pure and the perfect. That is why it is said, "we live in an illusion—a manmade delusion!"

But our true home is in this perfect reality, surrounded by the perfection that God himself intended for us. Know this, and believe it. Also know that this (perfect) reality interpenetrates and surrounds our (imperfect) reality and has an influence on everything therein. Due to this influence, everything is in a positive state of change, adjusting toward perfection. This continual process is called the Law of Adjustment. We should take comfort in this Law, for no matter how badly we mess things up, they are always being re-adjusted toward this unseen perfection.

See and feel, in your mind's eye, this great Law adjusting and correcting everything, even to the smallest detail. Know that you can LET GO and TRUST, at any time, back there in the imperfect world behind you.

Finally, with this feeling of absolute perfection radiating from the very pores of your being, step back through the dimensional window, back into the reality of the physical universe. Feel the shift in consciousness that has occurred and be assured that you have added a new dimension to your overall conscious awareness.

You will find it helpful to review this procedure each time before trying it again. Your mind will adjust itself to each portion, in a sequence that only it understands, and as more and more is incorporated it will recall other things that were previously overlooked.

In time you will be able to tune in "to the flow" at will, just by thinking about it—whether in or out of the meditation state. This will require many repetitions of the exercise however, to reinforce and strengthen the effect. By then you'll need only to recall the feeling to maintain yourself in that flow. And as you do so you'll be strengthening the connection to your higher self and maintaining the flow of Spirit into your life and affairs. The "charmed" state you've always longed for will be yours!

Please do not take this exercise lightly. It is very powerful and should be given priority in your meditative discipline. The results will be more than worth the effort.

In her book, *Innersource*, Kathleen Vande Kieft describes a vision she encountered during a moment of cosmic illumination:

"As I looked up I was startled to see that the ceiling and roof had dissolved, revealing the deep cerulean-blue sky above me and some wispy clouds. In that moment I perceived a heightened sense of reality where every color was brighter, every line distinct, and my mind crystal-clear. In this state of intense clarity a concept entered my mind, whole and intact, revealing to me the perfection of the universe.

"I saw how life was mapped out in intricate detail, to a scale so minute as to be incomprehensible. Every move, every person, every leaf on every tree, every situation, every millisecond, perfect to the finest detail... I saw how all the events in life, including and especially the painful ones, were glowing gifts of spirit ... I saw that life is planned in such perfection, resembling the intricate dance of the tiniest imaginable fly, with every form, every movement, every instant, progressing with mind-boggling precision."

Conclusion: Personal Truth

- ❖ Each person has a unique version of truth; it is something that each must uncover for themselves; it must be *lived* to fulfill individual destiny. We all have our own lessons to learn and by seeking our own truth we encounter what is needed. "To thine own self be true," is the whole of the law.
- ❖ Discovering one's personal truth is an ongoing process and is the most important pursuit in a person's life. Inner guidance must be trusted as infallible to steer one along the path of truth. What feels good is right; what feels bad is wrong (for you). Don't let the societal and religious concept of Conscience interfere -- anything done out of guilt or fear is wrong.
- ❖ Overindulgence must be avoided, even though it feels good initially. Anything with an obvious downside must be tempered with logic, awareness, and will.
- ❖ Never judge another for living their truth. In this vast free-will universe, all is allowed. Don't measure

another by your version of truth.
- ❖ Serve only one master: "A man who serves others serves a few, but he who lives his truth serves all humanity." (From an ancient Tibetan text.)

THE TRUE SELF:

- ❖ The invisible or hidden identity -- Inner Being. While we are physically focused, it acts as our guardian angel. Ever watchful, all-knowing and protective, it will assist in our endeavors if invited. It always seeks to guide, through the emotions, but will never interfere unless asked to do so specifically.
- ❖ The Inner Being is a god unto itself; it resides in a place of pure joy and has powers that are unlimited. As a projection of the hidden real God, it is our link to "All that is" and is our very own piece of divinity. No savior or intermediary is ever required.
- ❖ This higher self is not separated from us, it *is* us. In fact it is such an integral part, that without it we could not function. It is our awareness and will, and it provides the very life-force that we exist upon. It resides in the NOW and can be sensed through a "feeling state" devoid of thought.
- ❖ To get a sense of our whole Being, there are two aspects to consider: one is hidden, the other is visible. The hidden part is universal (part of the "All that is") it is the true essence of life. The visible part is focused in a specific time and place; it is learning lessons, developing character, and it provides individuality for the whole being. At death, the visible part withdraws to a higher dimension where it

continues life with fewer limitations, still learning and doing, but in closer contact with its Inner being.

INNER GUIDANCE:

- ❖ A continual source of communication from Inner Being that steers us infallibly toward personal truth and the fulfillment of our intentions. It communicates through feelings and emotions; sometimes through visions, omens, and the manipulation of physical (or mental) perceptions.
- ❖ Since we are always creating, Inner guidance gives constant feedback on whether or not we are creating what we truly want -- whether our creations are on a positive track, or if we're creating something we do not want. If we would monitor the trend of our thoughts, it always relays the appropriateness of present thought to what is wanted. When our thoughts make us feel pleasure and uplift us, we are creating in a positive direction; when they make us feel uneasy somehow, or give a sense of displeasure in ourselves, we are creating in a negative direction.
- ❖ Whenever our feelings alert us to mis-creating, we should stop the train of thought, then step back and ask ourself: "What do I want instead?" Realize that Inner guidance is telling you there's something important here -- and it's probably the opposite of what you're thinking. Determine what it is, then focus on that until the Law of Attraction builds thought momentum toward what is desired. When the feelings turn positive again, you're creating with momentum in a positive direction.

- ❖ To tell the difference between interfering Conscience and true Inner guidance, first determine if your feelings (which is the message from on high) are inspired from a sense of fear, guilt, or doubt. Conscience always guides by one of these three negative emotions. Inner guidance, on the other hand, will nudge you along with feelings of positive fulfillment -- much like the "carrot on a stick." It never seeks to frighten or scare.

NATURAL CREATIVITY:

- ❖ "Birds fly, fish swim, man creates," as Grandfather said. It is what man does naturally in the scheme of things. Most creation however is accomplished without the *conscious knowing* of its creators. We create blindly then expend great effort, in action, responding to our negative creations. We are always plugged into the creative flow, always creating. Our thoughts and their corresponding feelings fashion the reality we experience. Those thoughts and feelings we entertain most often -- and thereby experience -- *densify* into beliefs. Our beliefs act as automatic creative mechanisms that reproduce themselves in our experience; they rubber-stamp their likeness in a variety of ways, but always limit our reality to the status quo.
- ❖ The secret of creation is: : "*You get what you think about most, if you dwell on it with enough emotion, and if you think that it's possible.*" The Formula for the above is:

  THINK IT => FEEL IT => ALLOW IT ... IT IS!

- Allowing is a crucial ingredient, most often overlooked. Other ways to express the "feel" of allowing are: believing, expecting, permitting, having faith in, accepting the possibility of, letting it be.
- Emotion *is* the creative life-force. Its source is from Inner Being. Without it there would be no creations. If strongly elicited it speeds our creations into manifestation.
- The twin laws that assist man in all his creations are: The Law of Attraction and The Law of Change. These are probably the only laws that truly affect man. He is otherwise unlimited.

LAW OF ATTRACTION

states: "Like attracts like." "That which is like unto itself is drawn." "Birds of a feather flock together." This law gives density to our thoughts and feelings, causing them to manifest in our reality. Whatever we focus on or give our attention to, we make more of.

LAW OF CHANGE

states: that "all things must change with time." It could also be called the 'law of disintegration' because it breaks down (with time) what has been created; it makes room for newer and better creations. What we no longer give our attention to, we no longer give energy to -- unwanted creations are left to disintegrate naturally.

DELIBERATE CREATION:

- Once it is understood that we create all that we experience -- and we take full responsibility for it -- it is time to enter a whole new relationship with the world, as *conscious creators*. From this new perspective we let go the old concepts of luck, of odds and chance, of destiny and fate, and divine providence. In the old world these things were valid, because belief made them so. But in this higher worldview of self-destiny, we create exactly what <u>we</u> want, always following the promptings from Inner guidance, always on the path of personal truth.

- ❖ To create consciously we must reclaim all personal power surrendered to outside influences, especially to the mass mind of our particular culture. The first step is to question all *obvious* societal beliefs (usually disguised as good) testing them for personal truth with Inner guidance. Be wary of all beliefs that promote blind service to others, and "causes" that make you feel guilty for not acting. Realize that no one but you creates in your reality; that except for influence that you allow, your circle of personal reality is otherwise inviolable.
- ❖ A formula for deliberate creation can be derived from the first one. It is more powerful because it focuses more energy. By substituting 'want' for the ingredients 'think' and 'feel' in the original formula, we have the formula for deliberate creation:

WANT IT => ALLOW IT ... IT IS!

- ❖ Want is a powerful agent that stirs the creative forces into rapid motion. It combines thought and emotion into a focused thoughtform.
- ❖ There is however an even more potent agent than

want -- it's most literal translation in the terms of consciousness, is 'intent.' It combines 'want' and 'will' into an irresistible thoughtform that manifests rapidly. We now have what's called the Elixir of manifestation:

INTEND IT => ALLOW IT ... IT IS!

- ❖ An act of intention focuses the attention like a beam of light through a magnifying glass. If it is <u>clear</u> and unopposed by doubt, there is nothing to stop it from manifesting.
- ❖ A strong intent is the only thing that blocks harmful influence – either outer or inner.

CONTROLLING THOUGHT:

- ❖ Thought is the first essential element of any creation. There is nothing in creation that was not first born of thought. Since we are always creating (with thought) it is necessary to take control of our wandering thoughts -- especially important for *conscious creators*. The following techniques are useful tools to help discipline thought, while keeping us in the mode of creating positively toward what we want. These tools are called *Turn-abouts* because they change the direction of thought flow.

1) PROSPECTING

An abbreviation for pro-aspecting. Looking for the pro (or positive) aspect in everything encountered. Since there is good and bad in everything, what we focus on is what we draw out. Ignore the bad. There is a particular societal belief that says it's a cop-out to ignore a problem (to stick your head in the sand until it goes away) but that's exactly what must be done to change it, using this technique. Focus on the pleasing aspects instead.

2) THE REVERSAL

To be used whenever thoughts are spiraling out of control in a negative direction. The first alert comes from Inner guidance in the form of negative emotion. It's telling you, "Hey, look at what you're thinking -- I don't think we want to create this!" Step back and stop the thoughts. Ask yourself, "What do I want instead?" It is probably the opposite of what you've been thinking about. Identify what it is, then ask yourself, "Why do I want this?" As you dwell on the why's, you create clearer images and feelings of exactly what you do want. Soon, the Law of Attraction builds momentum and you're creating in a positive direction.

3) RE-CYCLING

- ❖ In everyday life we repeat numerous habitual actions, called event cycles; we do these the same way, at almost the same times, again and again. These habits lockup enormous stores of energy and limit our spontaneity (free-will choice). Once they are recognized, they can be unlocked and controlled. The energy freed can be recycled into new choices.
- ❖ You first have to identify (be aware of) the cycle and give it a name. Each time you begin the cycle, put forth the 'intent' of what you want instead, what

would better suit you. This act of intent, repeated at the start of the cycle will pre-pave the future, transforming the old cycle into a new one. It also blocks the influence of old habits and outworn beliefs.

- ❖ And don't just say the words (of your intent); you must see and feel exactly what you intend … and then allow.

ALLOWING:

- ❖ A truly magical state of Being. A state of mind devoid of negative emotion, discomfort, or need of any kind. The ultimate feel-good state of being. The fortunates who dwell in this place have unlimited freedom, continual joy, and a sense of total amazement with the world. *"In the whole world only a few people are awake, and they live in a state of total, constant amazement."*

- ❖ By allowing others to seek their own truth -- without judgment or prejudice -- we also allow ourselves. All the pain and limitation we experience in life is a direct result of not allowing ourselves. All judgment is self-judgment because we project our faults and bitterness, with our self, onto others. An allowing person can say with certainty: *"I am unique in all the world, I love what I am, and I allow all others to be what they are."*

- ❖ Allowing detaches us from all negatives in the world. Our attention to anything (perceived as) negative attaches us to that thing like a fly to a spider's web. By ignoring it, we deny it energy, and thereby deny it access to our reality. And allowing is not the same as tolerating -- to tolerate something causes a split of attention: half wants to ignore, but half is drawn back. That still binds us to it. To be free, we must allow!

- ❖ The belief in scarcity, and the guardedness it inspires, blocks an allowing attitude. The Universe is bountiful and friendly, with more than enough to satisfy every want of every person. But each individual must create for himself/ herself. Once this is realized, it becomes easier to allow.
- ❖ Allowing is a simple concept, with great potential rewards, but it is not easy for most people to master. Our society has raised us with too many irrational and limited beliefs -- causing us to be guarded -- they are difficult to shed because of peer pressure and manipulation by fear, guilt, and doubt. Those who break the mold will have to be courageous.

A FEEL-GOOD PHILOSOPHY:

- ❖ The bottom line is, whenever you feel good you are feeling your wholeness. You are in a place of allowing Inner Being to blend with your physical being. This speeds your personal vibrations and gives a noticeable high.
- ❖ What happens when you just feel good:
  1. You are closer to God, and connected to 'All-that-is.'
  2. You are aligned with and in the presence of Inner Being.
  3. You are 'in flow' with the wellspring of creative

essence.
4. You are protected; always in the right place at the right time.
5. You are in a place of health and well-being (the inner sanctuary).
6. You are creating in a positive direction, with positive momentum.
7. Your guidance is strong, in agreement with your thoughts.
8. You are closer to the true spirit of allowing.
9. You are self-empowered; nothing it seems, can be denied you.
10. It dissolves fear, guilt, and doubt from consciousness.

THERE IS NOTHING MORE IMPORTANT THAN TO FEEL GOOD!

❖ To make this a workable philosophy, the following should be done each day until a pattern of new habits emerge:
1. Intend each day on waking that you will seek out and identify those things that make you feel good. This is the same as seeking your personal truth. From now on, this is the single most important duty of the day.
2. Follow your guidance. Be sensitive to your feelings and trust them above all else -- even over logic. Use your feelings to monitor the trend of your thoughts, to alert you immediately when they (your thoughts) take you off-center.
3. Discipline your thoughts. Use the Reversal,

Prospecting, and Re-cycling at every opportunity. These not only train the mind, they keep your creations on a positive track.
4. Create what you want! Use the raw material of your daily seeking (for truth) to deliberately create your unique version of whatever is wanted. But always keep in mind the adage: "All things in moderation." Don't create more than you can manage.
5. ALLOW all others ... and ALLOW yourself!

BIBLIOGRAPHY

Castenada, Carlos. *The Teachings of Don Juan: A Yaqui Way of Knowledge.* Washington Square Press. 1985. **ISBN:** 0671600419

Finley, Guy. *The IntimateEnemy : Winning the War Within Yourself.* Llewellyn Pubns. 1997. **ISBN:** 1567182798

Howard, Vernon. *The Mystic Path To Cosmic Power.* New Life Foundation. 1999. **ISBN:** 0911203400

Howard, Vernon. *Psycho-Pictography.* New Life Foundation. 2001. **ISBN:** 0911203524

Kieft, Kathleen V. *Innersource*, Ballantine Books. 1988. **ISBN:** 0345346513

Roberts, Jane. *The Seth Material.* New Awareness Network. 2001. **ISBN:** 0971119805

www.ingramcontent.com/pod-product-compliance
Lightning Source LLC
Chambersburg PA
CBHW061331040426
42444CB00011B/2863